Jan Tschichold: Typographer

Ruari McLean

Jan Tschichold: Typographer

David R. Godine Boston

First U.S. edition published in 1975 by
David R. Godine, Publisher
306 Dartmouth Street
Boston, Massachusetts

Copyright © 1975 by Ruari McLean
ISBN 0–87923–160–2
LCC 75–13029

Book designed by Herbert Spencer and
Christine Charlton
Jacket designed by Ruari McLean, using Sabon and
Sabon Semi-bold

Text set in 12 on 14 point Monotype Garamond 156
Chapter headings in 24 point Sabon Semi-bold

The frontispiece photograph of Jan Tschichold
was taken in 1962 by Frank Bollingen

Made and printed in Great Britain by
Lund Humphries, Bradford and London

Contents

Appendices

Appendices 1–5 have been translated by Ruari McLean,

Appendix 3 with assistance from Darrell Hyder.

For Edith Tschichold

Foreword

When printing was invented in Europe in the fifteenth century, and replaced writing by hand as the commercial method for making books, it was an early example of industrial 'mass production'. But books were still hand-made. Each separate process that was necessary to print and bind an edition was controlled by the eyes, hands and hearts of craftsmen. Printing only started to become a truly mechanized industry at the end of the nineteenth century, especially when photographic methods of block- and plate-making put the old wood-engravers out of business in the 1880s; and it did not happen quickly. Many books were still being set by hand in the 1920s; it is only in the nineteen-sixties and seventies that printing plants in which no metal type exists have become the norm.

As long as books, journals and newspapers were all manufactured in more or less the same way, from type by means of hand or cylinder presses onto sheets of paper, typographic design remained the responsibility of the master printer, and was often left to the compositor. But as printing gradually became more complex and more specialized, and particularly when the introduction of mechanical punch-cutting in the early twentieth century enormously increased the number of type-faces available for printers, the separate profession of 'typographer' emerged. A typographer was someone who, in the first place, had studied the history of letter-forms, who could probably also draw them himself when necessary, and who could choose the most appropriate type-face not only for a given text but for a given set of conditions, from the ever-growing range of available faces. He could then so arrange the types on the pages that they would most effectively perform the function for which they were intended.

Charles Whittingham, and later Charles Jacobi, at the Chiswick Press in London, and Theodore Low De Vinne and Daniel Updike in America, were all typographic designers, but they were also master printers. Perhaps the first man to become an independent consultant typographer in the twentieth century was Bruce Rogers, who joined the Riverside Press in Cambridge, Massachusetts, in 1895. If several of the first typographers in the modern sense were Americans, it was probably because the two crucial inventions of mechanical composition, the Linotype and Monotype machines, were both developed in America. Another American, born five years earlier than Rogers, became the first freelance type designer: Frederick William Goudy, 1865–1947: by the time he died, he had designed over one hundred type-faces. Both Rogers and Goudy, and all their predecessors, were essentially book-men. Printing embraces not books only but every form of visual communication: newspapers, tickets, catalogues, journals, pamphlets, posters, telephone directories, maps, etc. Two men, both Europeans, did more than any others to take printing design into the twentieth century: they were Stanley Morison (1889–1967) and Jan Tschichold (1902–74).

Morison's greatest influence on the world of printing was through the British Monotype Corporation and the programme of type-faces they made available on his advice from 1922 onwards – the best known being Morison's own 'Times New Roman' which appeared in 1932, was only superseded, for setting *The Times* newspaper, in 1972 and which is still used in numerous periodical publications all over the world.

Tschichold's influence was first exercised entirely on the Continent; but he worked twice in England. First briefly in 1935, when he was invited by Lund Humphries of Bradford, then publishers of *The Penrose Annual*, to exhibit examples of his work in their London office, redesign their stationery, and design a volume of *Penrose*; second, in 1947, when he was invited by Allen Lane to re-organize the typographic design of the entire list of Penguin Books. This required three years and made him as well known and influential in Britain and the United States as he had been on the Continent. The present work is an attempt to define his typographical achievement, to describe his teaching and to consider his total typographic influence, an influence which has affected all English-speaking peoples.

Most of the translations of Tschichold's writings included in this work have been made by the present writer, with much help from Fianach Lawry. I must also thank Alfred Fairbank for the loan of valuable material and for permission to quote from his correspondence with Tschichold; Rudolf Hostettler for permission to quote a letter written to him by Tschichold; John Taylor, Charlotte Burri, Berthold Wolpe, and my wife, for help and advice on many occasions; and my American publisher, David Godine, for constructive criticisms of my text. Tschichold's young assistant at Penguin Books in 1948, Erik Frederiksen,

The terms 'A4' and 'A5' have been used in the text to denote book page sizes of 297 × 210 mm (11·6 × 8·2 in.) and 210 × 148 mm (8·2 × 5·8 in.) respectively. These are in the DIN range of International Paper sizes, in use in Germany throughout Tschichold's working life, and more recently adopted in Britain and many other countries, but not used in the USA. In all page measurements, depth precedes width.

now a leading typographer in Denmark, most kindly wrote a short account of his association with Tschichold specially for this book. This has been incorporated in Chapter 5, a contribution for which I here record my appreciation. For other help and information, I wish to thank Eleanor Steiner-Prag, Michael Twyman, Hans Schmoller, John Dreyfus, Darrell Hyder, and Herbert Spencer – whose design of the book also gives me great pleasure.

Finally, for his friendship and teaching over more than thirty years, quite apart from the help he gave me with this book, I am deeply grateful to Jan Tschichold himself. It is a profound grief that he died a year before its publication.

Chapter 1   Modern typography

Who invented, or first practised, 'modern typography'? What *is* 'modern typography'? Without the quotation marks, the words have no particular meaning, since no one style exists, or ever has existed, that is more 'modern' than any other. There is good typography and bad typography, but not modern typography in any significant sense. 'Modern typography', in quotes, can be equated with a particular movement known in Germany as 'Die neue Typographie'. This was the title of Jan Tschichold's book, published in Berlin in 1928, which defined and described it. What 'Die neue Typographie' actually was cannot be exactly or briefly stated, since it meant different things to different people; but, as proposed by Tschichold, it was a radically new attitude to typography in printing. It rejected decoration, it had to be strictly functional, it was an expression of the new age of the machine, it was simple and pure, it was universal. It was the way that printing had to be done in the twentieth century. It was revolutionary, and for some artists its philosophy seemed to harmonize with the philosophy of the Communist Revolution.

It was asymmetric, because symmetry involved putting words and sentences into shapes which were decorative and artificial, and had nothing to do with their meaning, and were therefore false. Asymmetry, also, was 'dynamic' and not 'static'; it was therefore in harmony with the age. Its type-face was sans serif, because in sans (or so it was claimed) the forms of letters were shorn of inessentials and stripped down to their basic, elemental shapes.

Tschichold was the first to formulate these theories into a system and to show how the 'modernist' movement in art could be related to ordinary printing. Printing, like architecture, touches every civilized person at almost every point of their lives, and Tschichold, working in Germany up to 1933, took daily printing, or at least a large part of it, into the twentieth century. But where did

Tschichold's ideas come from? He was certainly not the first exponent of the kind of typography he was preaching.

Asymmetry had been used on the title-pages and chapter headings of books made by designers in London such as Laurence Housman, Charles Ricketts and Charles Shannon during the 1890s: they were part of a 'modern' movement dissatisfied with the aesthetics and ethics of the nineteenth century, just as William Morris was, but they did not reject the machine. The title-page of Bernard Shaw's *Plays: Pleasant and Unpleasant*, 1898, is an exercise in plain asymmetric typography, by Shaw himself, very close to what the Bauhaus and Tschichold were doing twenty years later, and based on the same rationalistic approach. Theodore Low De Vinne's *Title-pages as seen by a printer*, New York, 1901, actually has a chapter on 'The Ragged Title', taking the off-centre style back to B.C. Greek coins and old medals, and showing off-centre title-pages by Charles Jacobi of the Chiswick Press in 1892 and Will Bradley in Chicago in 1893; but he condemned the style as a trick, apparently without understanding that there were serious theories behind it.

Jacques Damase, in *Révolution typographique*, Geneva, 1966, traces the modern movement in typography back to Stéphane Mallarmé (and indeed, even further back) but he starts his book with the words: 'The strange poem that appeared in May 1897 in London in the revue *Cosmopolis* "Un coup de dés jamais n'abolira le hazard"[1] can be considered historically as the first shot from the cannon that woke the spirit of the modern book.' Then there followed Kandinsky, Marinetti, the Futurists, the Constructivists, Apollinaire, Braque, Picasso, Dada and, most important, Moholy-Nagy and Lissitzky: all of whom, with many others, contributed ideas to 'Die neue Typographie'. None of them were, however, effective or useful as practical typographers.

Many artists were using letters, words, and typographic material (e.g. printing types, wood-letter, rules, small and large dots, etc.) in new ways; they were 'painting pictures' with them, creating images which could not be *read* but only apprehended, by intuition and imagination. They were exploring the boundaries of what could be expressed on paper by printed images. They were testing the book as a medium of expression, to see what more could be done with it. Lissitzky's famous manifesto 'Topography of typography', published in the periodical *Merz*, at Hanover, in July 1923, ended with the sentences:[2]

7. The new book demands the new writer. Ink-stand and goose-quill are dead.
8. The printed page transcends space and time. The printed page, the infinity of the book, must be transcended.
THE ELECTRO LIBRARY

[1] The original, with Mallarmé's corrections, is in the Harvard College Library.

[2] Lissitzky wrote in German. His actual words were:
"7. Das neue Buch fordert den neuen Schriftsteller. Tintenfass und Gänsekiel sind tot.
8. Der gedruckte Bogen überwindet Raum und Zeit. Der gedruckte Bogen, die Unendlichkeit der Bücher, muss überwunden werden. Die Elektrobibliothek."
The translation is that used in Sophie Lissitzky-Küppers' *El Lissitzky*, Thames & Hudson, London, 1968.

Whatever they achieved, they did not make any discoveries that improved, or in any way altered, the design of books as a medium for conveying a writer's words to a reader. Typography is not an art in its own right: an artist who makes images with typographic material is not a typographer. Typography is the means by which written words are conveyed in the most direct, economic and unbiased way to readers, making the best (i.e. the most effective) use of contemporary printing techniques. Typography is a servant, to author and reader, not a master. It must also be remembered that typography is not concerned only with books, but with every kind of printed communication, including newspapers, magazines, catalogues, timetables, posters and bus tickets – all the endless miscellany of print used in modern civilization.

Another important aspect of typography, often overlooked, is its integral dependence on the techniques of printing. Typographic design is conditioned by the kind of printing being used; a designer designs specifically for an intended process and materials, just as an architect designs for steel, glass, stone or bricks.

At the turn of the last century, printing techniques, which had been changing slowly throughout the nineteenth century, began to change much more rapidly and fundamentally. From the 1880s, photographic methods of block-making revolutionized all printed illustration, a very far-reaching revolution indeed, with which some artists, like Aubrey Beardsley and the Robinson brothers in England, quickly came to terms, while others did not. At the same time the four-colour process revolutionized and debased colour printing. (Photography, invented in the 1840s, had already made it necessary to rethink the whole basis of the art of painting. What was an artist, what was a designer?) Mechanical composition on the Monotype and Linotype machines revolutionized printers' composition methods during the first quarter of the new century. The use of the pantograph, with mechanical methods of type manufacture, led to the introduction of hundreds of new type-faces, giving the designer of printed matter choices and problems that had never before existed.

The Industrial Revolution not only changed manufacturing methods, temporarily abolished craftsmanship and caused grave deterioration in nearly every visual aspect of the environment: it also gave rise to dramatic social problems, problems which increased in geometric progression with the population explosion of the nineteenth century and made upheaval inevitable. The catastrophe of the First World War increased the urgent need for reform; a mood of desperation, even violence, grew among many artists and designers who early saw how much had to be thrown out before new things could be substituted.

There is no moment of time at which 'modern typography' can be said to have been invented. Thought is continuous: the conceptions of the Bauhaus can be traced backwards to Peter Behrens, who taught Gropius, to earlier designers like Christopher Dresser, even to Henry Cole and his 'modern' designs for Minton china, and as much further back as one cares to go. Whatever its antecedents, a revolutionary attitude to the visual arts was in the air over all Europe – and in America too – in the first quarter of the twentieth century. Mackintosh's Glasgow School of Art, conceived in 1896, was a building of the twentieth century: 'his style', wrote Andrew McLaren Young in 1968, 'is the style of the future'.[3] In 1900, T. J. Cobden-Sanderson at his Doves Press was evolving a typographic style of extreme simplicity, in his quest for the 'Book Beautiful', which was closer to Tschichold's style twenty-five years later, than to William Morris's in the 1890s. In 1917, Theo van Doesburg, with Van der Leck, Mondrian, Huszar, Kok and Oud, formed in Holland the group they named 'de Stijl', with many of the same ideals. In 1919 Walter Gropius founded the Bauhaus at Weimar; and by 1924 examples of practical typography discernible as totally 'modern' can be found from many places in Europe, e.g. in designs by Kurt Schwitters in Hanover, Walter Dexel in Jena, Joost Schmidt and Herbert Bayer in Weimar, Henryk Berlewi in Warsaw, and Jan Tschichold in Leipzig. It must be said here that the Bauhaus itself made little contribution to the advancement of typographic design. Herbert Bayer, first a pupil, then an instructor at the Bauhaus, and the man whose name is most closely identified with its typography, was trained as an architect, and has practised as architect, exhibition designer, graphic designer, industrial designer, sculptor, painter and mural painter. His architecture and environment designs at Aspen, Colorado, against a backcloth of mountains, are memorably beautiful. But he was never a typographer. His idea of a universal type, with one alphabet only, drawn in 1925 – an experiment also carried out by Tschichold (see pp.42–3), and others – was certainly worth making; it ought to have taught him, as it taught others, that capital letters, like punctuation marks, are functional in typography, since they signal the beginnings of sentences, proper names, different meanings of words, and so on. To omit capital letters entirely makes printed matter more difficult to read. Yet the catalogue of the great Bauhaus Exhibition in 1968, designed by Bayer, was printed entirely in sans serif without capitals – showing a determination to ignore the axiom that typographic design is a *servant* to communication.

Of all early practitioners of 'modern typography', Tschichold was, as far as I can ascertain, the only one whose earliest training was in lettering and calligraphy. Because of this he understood more clearly than others what was involved in typographic communication through the medium of the printing-press. He was the first to offer a coherent philosophy of design by which all typographic problems – not just books, but magazines, newspapers, and all the clutter of commercial, day-to-day printed ephemera – could be tackled in ways that were rational, suited to modern production techniques, and aesthetically satisfying.

[3] *Charles Rennie Mackintosh*. Exhibition Catalogue published by Edinburgh Festival Society Ltd, 1968.

Chapter 2   Early days 1902-26

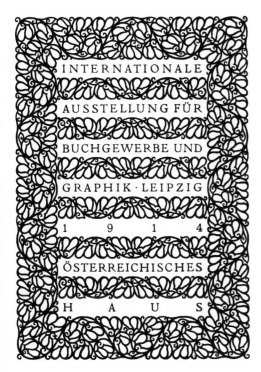

Cover design (not by Tschichold) of the International Printing Exhibition ('Bugra'), Leipzig, 1914. Reduced: original in orange and black on white paper.

1 Much of the information in this chapter is drawn from the article on (and by) Tschichold which appeared in *Typographische Monatsblätter*, No.4, 1972.

Jan Tschichold[1] was born on 2 April 1902 in Leipzig, the eldest son of a sign painter and lettering artist, Franz Tschichold, and his wife Maria (née Zapff). His father's parents lived in Pförten near Forst in Niederlausitz, a Germanized part of Wenden- or Sorbenland. The Sorben people are West-Slavs: Tschichold was ethnologically a Slav, related to the Czechs, and had an inborn sympathy with Czech graphic art.

His father's profession made him familiar, from childhood, with many kinds of painted lettering. In helping his father, he learned about lettering, without deciding to make it his own profession. He wanted to become an artist. His parents felt that this was too uncertain a livelihood; as a compromise, it was decided that he would become a teacher of drawing. As further education was then already required in Saxony for this profession, the fourteen-year-old boy was sent to the Teacher Training College at Grimma, near Leipzig.

An event which occurred a few years earlier had already given him some experience with the arts of the book. This was the International Exhibition of the Graphic Arts (Internationale Ausstellung für Buchgewerbe und Graphik, shortened to 'Bugra') at Leipzig in 1914, where he saw well-designed books and type-faces. The earliest example of good typography that actually attracted him was an issue of *Zwiebelfisch* (*Printer's Pie*), a 'Journal of Books and other things', which he bought in a Leipzig bookshop in April 1914 for 60 pfennig. At that time he could hardly afford to buy books at 20 pfennig each. This periodical, set and printed by Poeschel & Trepte, made a deep impression on him. He had already, aged twelve, so disliked the title lettering of a Brentano novel picked up at the University Bookshop that he had attempted to redraw it in pen and ink in the style of Poeschel & Trepte's lettering in *Zwiebelfisch*. The typography of the Brentano novel also displeased him, but he did not yet know how to improve it.

In August 1914 the Great War broke out. 'Bugra' closed its doors, but the 'Hall of Culture', a great domed building with a splendid exhibition of the history of civilisation, remained open. Equipped with a season ticket, the twelve-year-old Tschichold spent hundreds of hours of his spare time acquainting himself with the civilisations of the past and the story of books and lettering – subjects which his school could not teach him. Here it was all displayed, with an exceptionally fine descriptive catalogue as well. The 'Hall of Culture' and its catalogue laid the foundations of Tschichold's education.

At Grimma, he pursued the study of lettering in his free time. He devoured Edward Johnston's *Writing and Illuminating, and Lettering*, of which Bernard Newdigate wrote in 1938: 'I well remember how when I visited the Exhibition [at Leipzig] in July of 1914, I seemed to see in the German Pavilions the hand of Johnston on every stall and every wall; for his book, translated into German by his pupil Anna Simons, and his teaching and practice, had an influence on German book production far exceeding that which it enjoyed in England;[2] he also studied Rudolf von Larisch's *Ornamental Lettering* and did much calligraphic writing with a broad-nibbed pen. It was at this time that his interest in the early punch-cutters began. A page of his lettering survives from this period, showing the capitals and small letters of an Italic which might be Granjon. The letters, not all of them completely finished, were taken, without enlargement, from an old work probably of the early seventeenth century. For a beginner of sixteen, it is creditable. Neither Johnston nor Larisch in their textbooks mention the beauty of the old type specimens. Both were letterers, not type designers, and had had no experience of type-designing. The general level of lettering and design at that time in German books, newspapers, magazines and general printing was deplorable.

Tschichold already realized, without being told, that there was a need for new and better letter-forms and type-faces – hence the exercise in drawing italic. At the time, he was also impressed by a text-face (it may have been Caslon or Imprint), which he saw in an English magazine.

At the Grimma Training College, Tschichold found himself more and more attracted to the idea of becoming a type designer. His parents finally gave their consent, and it was decided that after three years study at Grimma he should go to the Academy for the Graphic Arts and the Book Production Trade at Leipzig.

His studies at Grimma had given him a good knowledge of French and, more important, Latin. His knowledge of Latin was of incalculable help in his later studies of type design; he often regretted that he never learned Greek. He did not learn much English until he worked in England, many years later.

[2] *The Art of the Book*, The Studio, London, 1938.

In the spring of 1919, Jan Tschichold was accepted, despite his youth (he was then seventeen), into the class of Professor Hermann Delitsch, and there learned calligraphy, engraving, etching, wood-engraving, and book-binding. He soon became a favoured pupil; Delitsch told Tschichold there was not much more that he could teach him, and gave him a free hand. Delitsch was above all a calligrapher and authority on the history of the European book hands, and was perhaps a little looked down upon by the other teachers, because he was not an 'artist', like them. But he knew much more than they, and introduced the young Tschichold to the writing masters of the Italian Renaissance, like Palatino and Tagliente, and to the Dutchman Jan van de Velde (1605). Tschichold did not discover Arrighi until much later.

While still at Grimma, Tschichold corresponded with Heinrich Wieynck, a Dresden type designer and sometime Conservator of the Art Gallery Library. After two years' study in Leipzig, he went to the School of Arts and Crafts at Dresden, for further study, partly under Wieynck. After a year, however, he returned to Leipzig to continue under Delitsch. In 1921, aged nineteen, he was appointed by Walter Tiemann (1876–1951), Director of the Leipzig Academy, to be assistant in charge of the evening classes in lettering at the Academy. He also became a special student of Tiemann's and was given his own small studio in the Academy. Much was being heard then of Rudolf Koch (1876–1934) at Offenbach, regarded as at the opposite end of the pole from Leipzig Academy. His small, beautifully lithographed manuscript of Ernst Moritz Arndt's *Vom Vaterland* (Gerstung, Offenbach am Main, 1913) had caught Tschichold's eye at 'Bugra', and he had bought a copy, costing 8 marks, with some carefully saved pocket money. Koch's Maximilian Gothic, then the only new type-face in Germany, impressed Tschichold. He made one or two trips to Offenbach to make the acquaintance of the revered master himself. Koch had at that time come under the influence of the Expressionists. His lettering was for a short time used as a model by Tschichold, but not for long.

During these years, Tschichold made industrious use of the library and print collection of the Master Printers' Federation Library in Leipzig, and spent countless hours there. He was allowed to think of himself as the sole inheritor of all its fabulous treasures, which in fact he was, since no other visitor but himself had been seen in its reading-rooms for years. The Library Catalogue alone contains 1406 pages. Hardly anything of this great collection remains today. There he made himself familiar with the type specimens of Simon-Pierre Fournier the Younger, many other old type specimen books and a great number of the old writing masters, incunable pages and other treasures.

He began at this time to collect such items himself. This was not as difficult as it

had been earlier since he now had regular commissions from Erich Gruner, a Leipzig artist, to design advertisements for the Leipzig Trade Fairs. Between 1921 and 1925 he drew, calligraphically, many hundreds of these advertisements. At that time, these were never set in type, nor did anyone think that they should be. The only possible type-faces were 'Ohio' and 'Cheltenham' (known also as 'Sorbonne') which even at that time Tschichold did not like. The accepted opinion was that only specially drawn lettering could look beautiful.

Setting had to be done in bold or ultra bold faces, a reaction against the enfeebled and spidery typography of the 1890s, and even Tiemann's Medieval seemed to look old-fashioned by then. That it was possible to do good work with normal, not bold face, types was a concept that had not yet been grasped. The poorly-designed type-faces then readily available were used in horrible

Leipziger Messe

Allgemeine Mustermesse mit
Technischer Messe und
Baumesse

Die allgemeine internationale
Messe Deutschlands

Die erste und größte Messe der Welt.
Für Aussteller und Einkäufer
gleich wichtig.

BEGINN DER HERBSTMESSE AM 27. AUGUST 1922.

Auskunft erteilt und Anmeldungen nimmt entgegen
MESSAMT FÜR DIE MUSTERMESSEN
IN LEIPZIG

DIE IDEE VND DAS EWIGE SIND DAS MASSGEBENDE NICHT IRGEND EIN MENSCH ODER IRGEND EINE ZEIT

Lettering by Tschichold, 1923. Reduced. Original
in black only.

22

Lettering by Tschichold, 1923. Reduced. Original
in black, red, and blue.

combinations; any sense of typographic discipline was completely lacking. Until about 1895, the setting of advertising and jobbing work, if not in any real sense beautiful, had at least been pretty and neat. The work of Carl Poeschel (1874–1944) and Karl Klingspor (1868–1950) was always admired by Tschichold, but he considered it later to have been without general influence. The 'book-artists' in effect knew little about typography and could hardly use their own individual type-faces. Emil Rudolf Weiss (1875–1943) still marked corrections to his (by today's standards quite inadequate) layouts in millimetres, not points, when he wanted more or less space, or just wrote 'a bit higher' or 'a bit lower'.

Stanley Morison was not yet at work with the Monotype Corporation, and so the new cutting of Garamond was not yet available. Bodoni was newly available for machine composition.

Tschichold's interest in typography and type design increased. He worked for a short time with Poeschel & Trepte, who gave him his first practical experience of type-setting, and later, as a freelance, for Fischer & Wittig. A great event for him at this time was the discovery of the prospectus for Charles Enschedé's *Fonderies de Caractères* (an expensive work which had been published in Haarlem in 1908). In it he found a splendid page set in the Textura of Henric de Lettersnider (about 1490) and printed from brand new type, sharper than in the book itself, which he could not afford to buy until 1933. Closer examination opened his eyes to the niceties of type-cutting. He designed at this time a gothic type, of which only the first sketches have survived. It was not an historical reproduction nor did it show the influence of either Koch or Weiss.

The advertisement for the printing firm of Fischer & Wittig in Leipzig of 1923 is interesting, because it is the first documentation of his practical knowledge of the writing books of Arrighi and Tagliente.[3] The lettering is clearly the fruit of Tschichold's studies of these and other writing masters. The inside pages of the card shown had to be set in 'Ohio', because no better type-face was available.

The illustration of the hand-drawn Insel-Verlag advertisement is one of three such items shown by Tschichold at the International Exhibition of Modern Calligraphic Art in Vienna, April–May 1926, at which the English exhibitors included Edward Johnston, Eric Gill, Graily Hewitt and Alfred Fairbank – who later became a close friend by correspondence.

In the 'visual' arts the 'isms' were chasing one another in quick succession. In 1923 Expressionism was dying. Tschichold heard the term 'Suprematism' mentioned, and perhaps also 'Constructivism', and since he could find no-one else to explain these words to him, went to the art historian of the Academy, who

[3] Morison was writing an italic hand at least by 1919: see N. Barker, *Stanley Morison*, Macmillan, London, 1972, p.83.

25 Jahre

Insel-Verlag

1899 * 1924

Advertisement drawn by Tschichold (signed I T)
for Insel-Verlag, 1924. Reduced. Original in black
and red. The trademark was drawn by Peter
Behrens.

had never heard of them. Good advice was hard to find. However, Tschichold managed somehow to discover a little about these new movements. When the Weimar Bauhaus held its first Exhibition, in August 1923, he went to see it and came back deeply impressed.

He was then twenty-one, open-minded, and seething with ideas. Here was something absolutely new. For some time the 'Jugendstil' of his parents' home had stuck in his throat. Now, to see modern art and design spread out before him, and applied to type and book design as well as everything else, was a real shock. Perhaps, for a short time, he was also confused by the amount of historical knowledge, picked up quickly, and not yet absorbed. Whatever the point of departure was, he flung himself enthusiastically into the pursuit of the new.

DIE BÜCHER DES INSEL-VERLAGS

gehen nicht aus billiger Massen-
fabrikation hervor·Sie erstreben in Papier,
Druck und Einband höchste Leistung·Sie
wollen nicht blenden, sondern dauern·

Insel-Bücherei ⟨ der Band 1 M ⟩·Vier Mark-Bücher·
Bibliothek der Romane ⟨ der Band 5 M ⟩·Briefbücher und
Memoiren · Illustrierte und Kunstbücher · Goethe-Bücher·
Deutsche Klassiker auf Dünndruckpapier·Gesamtausgaben
von Balzac, Dickens, Dostojewski, Shakespeare, Tolstoi·
Werke zeitgenössischer Dichter

DIE BÜCHER SIND HIER VORRÄTIG

He had seen, at Weimar, the work of Herbert Bayer (who was a student there from 1921 to 1923, and who designed in 1923 the cover of the first Bauhaus book, *Staatliches Bauhaus in Weimar 1919–1923*), Josef Albers, Alfred Arndt, Marcel Breuer, Lyonel Feininger, Walter Gropius, Hans Itten, Wassily Kandinsky, Paul Klee, Gerhard Marcks, Laszlo Moholy-Nagy, Georg Muche, Hinnerk Scheper, Oskar Schlemmer, Joost Schmidt, Lothar Schreyer, and Gunta Stadler-Stölzl. He soon became aware of, and met, El Lissitzky, the Russian who had already influenced and inspired the graphic side of the Bauhaus; Theo van Doesburg, one of the founders of 'De Stijl', who taught in Weimar from 1921 to 1923 and also influenced the Bauhaus; Kurt Schwitters, a Dadaist and pioneer of modern typography; Piet Zwart, first an architect and then a typographer; Man Ray, the painter and photographer; and John Heartfield (born Helmut Herzfelde), another

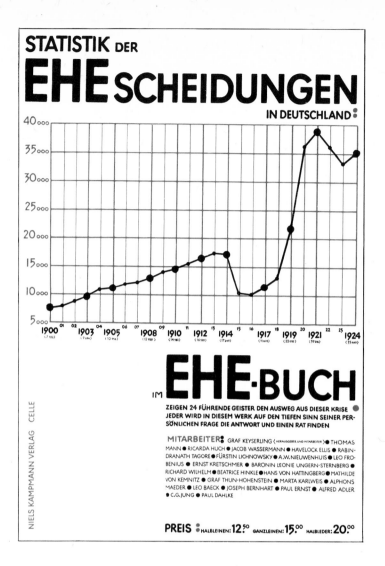

Dadaist, who changed his name in Berlin in 1916 to John Heartfield as a protest against the war, and who with George Grosz pioneered photo-montage caricatures. These were only a few, but the leaders, of the 'modern' movement then sparking and hissing all over Europe: the names and work of many others appear in the articles and books which Tschichold wrote during the next few years.

The poster for the Warsaw publisher Philobiblon, 1924, shows a totally new Tschichold: design, instead of art. The type consists entirely of the sans serif available in the composing-room. It was not chosen without much thought. Lettering was excluded.

Under the influence of Laszlo Moholy-Nagy's and El Lissitzky's paintings and designs with their balance and tension of strongly contrasting abstract forms, the

Letterheading designed by Tschichold for a
dancer, 1925. Original in black and terracotta.

Weimar Bauhaus Exhibition, and his disenchantment with the wretched
typography of his time, Tschichold came to believe that salvation lay in
abandoning the rule that setting must be symmetrical, and in declaring that
sans serif (then still called Grotesque) was the only right type for every kind of
job. His manifesto, published in October 1925 in the Leipzig *Typographische
Mitteilungen* under the title of 'Elementare Typographie' ('The Principles of
Typography'), ran as follows:

1. The new typography is purposeful.
2. The purpose of all typography is communication.
Communication must be made in the shortest, simplest, most definite way.
3. For typography to perform its social function, there must be *organization* of its
component parts, both *internal* (i.e. content) and *external* (consistent use of printing
methods and materials).

Left: Jan Tschichold, 1920.

Right: An early typographic poster designed by Tschichold for Philobiblon, publisher in Warsaw, 1924. Reduced. Black and gold on white card with black border. The text means 'Books from Philobiblon in Warsaw can be had here'.

4. *Internal organization* is restriction to the basic elements of typography: letters, figures, signs, lines of type set by hand and by machine.

The basic elements of the new typography include, in the visually organized world, the exact picture: photography. The basic type form is *sans serif* in all its variations: light, medium, bold, narrow to expanded.

Types with definite style characteristics or of nationalistic flavour, like Gothic, Fraktur, or 'Kirchenslavic', are not simple enough in form, and tend to restrict the possibilities of international communication.

Of all the many varieties of type-faces in use today, 'Roman' is the most familiar. For many kinds of work, although it is not truly simple enough in form, it is potentially more readable than many sans serifs.

The aims of this revolution were simplicity and clarity – both conspicuously lacking in the typography of 1925.

Tschichold, the only one of all the 'modernist' designers already mentioned who had been trained in lettering and calligraphy, was the first to rationalize and formulate the new ideas into systems which could be applied to everyday printing. He was the first who spoke to, and could be understood by, the ordinary printer.

His manifesto, 'Elementare Typographie', had an immediate effect, and was widely discussed. Every compositor in the country learned the name Tschichold. His proposals were passionately praised and equally passionately condemned, but

KSIĄŻKI

WYDAWNICTWA

PHILOBIBLON

w WARSZAWIE

TUTAJ DO NABYCIA

31

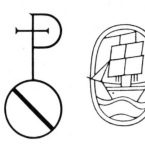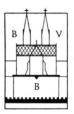

Symbols designed by Tschichold. From left to right:
Poeschel & Trepte, Leipzig, 1927.
Insel-Verlag, Leipzig, 1931.
Der Bücherkreis, Berlin, 1931.
Edith Tschichold, 1951.
Birkhäuser Verlag, Basle, 1941.
Burg-Verlag, Basle, 1942.
Heinrich Majer Verlag, Basle, 1951.
F. Hoffmann-La Roche, Basle, 1957.

in a few years the results began to be seen. Type ornaments and ugly old-fashioned type-faces gradually disappeared. The domination of the centred layout was on the wane: a great cleaning-up was in progress.

Tschichold sought to make himself independent and at the end of 1925 went to Berlin to set up as a freelance designer. He had already designed many bindings and title-pages for Insel-Verlag in Leipzig. In Berlin he married Edith, née Kramer, training to become a journalist, whom he had met a year earlier, in Leipzig. Then a letter arrived from Paul Renner, engaged in establishing the German Master Printers' School in Munich, who wished to recommend Tschichold for the teaching post Renner had occupied in Frankfurt am Main. The result of their correspondence was that Renner invited Tschichold to become a teacher in the Munich School: Renner was then heavily involved with his 'Futura' type-face and hoped that Tschichold's appointment would further his own efforts in Munich. So on 1 June 1926, aged 24, Tschichold went to Munich and took up the teaching of the Master Printer and Trade courses in typography and calligraphy. From 1926 to 1933 he taught at least thirty hours each week. His classes consisted of not less than twenty-five students and he gave individual instruction to them all.

Chapter 3   Work in Germany 1927-32

In Munich, Tschichold continued to widen his experience and reputation as a freelance designer. He was constantly testing the validity of the beliefs expressed in his manifesto of 1925. Examples of his work at this time are shown on pp.34–55. Probably the best-known and most influential of his designs of this period are his film posters for the Munich 'Phoebus Palace', then deservedly admired and now poster classics. (Today, one feels that the film business seems to have given up even trying to produce posters worthy of films which are themselves often works of art.) Tschichold used only type (usually but not always sans serif), geometrical shapes, photographs and flat colours (mostly the strong combination of black and red) to make designs of great impact, originality and elegance. The new vision of the artists whom Tschichold admired, like Man Ray, Lissitzky and Moholy-Nagy, was here given practical application.

Apart from the posters, he designed personal and commercial letter-headings and other small typographic jobs, and wrote and designed his own books. Tschichold was also still designing and drawing spine title-panels for Insel-Verlag books, which he had begun doing in Leipzig, in a traditional centred style.

His first book, *Die neue Typographie*, was published in Berlin in the summer of 1928. (The price before 1 June was 5 marks; after that the price was 6.50 marks.)

It was, in a very literal sense, epoch-making for it was the first publication in any language to attempt to lay down principles of typographic design which could be applied to the whole printing trade, embracing jobbing, advertising and journals, as well as books. The New York printer T. L. De Vinne's excellent series of four volumes published between 1900 and 1910 under the general title of

VORZUGS-ANGEBOT

Im VERLAG DES BILDUNGSVERBANDES der Deutschen Buchdrucker,
Berlin SW 61, Dreibundstr. 5, erscheint demnächst:

JAN TSCHICHOLD
Lehrer an der Meisterschule für Deutschlands Buchdrucker in München

DIE NEUE TYPOGRAPHIE

**Handbuch für die gesamte Fachwelt
und die drucksachenverbrauchenden Kreise**

Das Problem der neuen gestaltenden Typographie hat eine lebhafte
Diskussion bei allen Beteiligten hervorgerufen. Wir glauben dem Bedürf-
nis, die aufgeworfenen Fragen ausführlich behandelt zu sehen, zu ent-
sprechen, wenn wir jetzt ein Handbuch der **NEUEN TYPOGRAPHIE**
herausbringen.

Es kam dem Verfasser, einem ihrer bekanntesten Vertreter, in diesem
Buche zunächst darauf an, den engen Zusammenhang der neuen
Typographie mit dem **Gesamtkomplex heutigen Lebens** aufzuzei-
gen und zu beweisen, daß die neue Typographie ein ebenso notwendi-
ger Ausdruck einer neuen Gesinnung ist wie die neue Baukunst und
alles Neue, das mit unserer Zeit anbricht. Diese geschichtliche Notwendigkeit der neuen Typographie belegt weiterhin eine kritische Darstellung der **alten Typographie**. Die Entwicklung der **neuen Malerei**, die für alles Neue unserer Zeit geistig bahnbrechend gewesen ist,
wird in einem reich illustrierten Aufsatz des Buches leicht faßlich dar-
gestellt. Ein kurzer Abschnitt „**Zur Geschichte der neuen Typographie**" leitet zu dem wichtigsten Teile des Buches, den **Grundbegriffen
der neuen Typographie** über. Diese werden klar herausgeschält,
richtige und falsche Beispiele einander gegenübergestellt. Zwei wei-
tere Artikel behandeln „**Photographie und Typographie**" und
„**Neue Typographie und Normung**".

Der Hauptwert des Buches für den Praktiker besteht in dem zweiten
Teil „**Typographische Hauptformen**" (siehe das nebenstehende
Inhaltsverzeichnis). Es fehlte bisher an einem Werke, das wie dieses Buch
die schon bei einfachen Satzaufgaben auftauchenden gestalterischen
Fragen in gebührender Ausführlichkeit behandelte. Jeder Teilabschnitt
enthält neben **allgemeinen typographischen Regeln** vor allem die
Abbildungen aller in Betracht kommenden **Normblätter** des Deutschen
Normenausschusses, alle andern (z. B. postalischen) **Vorschriften** und
zahlreiche Beispiele, Gegenbeispiele und Schemen.

Für jeden Buchdrucker, insbesondere jeden Akzidenzsetzer, wird „Die
neue Typographie" ein **unentbehrliches Handbuch** sein. Von nicht
geringerer Bedeutung ist es für Reklamefachleute, Gebrauchsgraphiker,
Kaufleute, Photographen, Architekten, Ingenieure und Schriftsteller,
also für alle, die mit dem Buchdruck in Berührung kommen.

INHALT DES BUCHES

Werden und Wesen der neuen Typographie
Das neue Weltbild
Die alte Typographie (Rückblick und Kritik)
Die neue Kunst
Zur Geschichte der neuen Typographie
Die Grundbegriffe der neuen Typographie
Photographie und Typographie
Neue Typographie und Normung

Typographische Hauptformen
Das Typosignet
Der Geschäftsbrief
Der Halbbrief
Briefhüllen ohne Fenster
Fensterbriefhüllen
Die Postkarte
Die Postkarte mit Klappe
Die Geschäftskarte
Die Besuchskarte
Werbsachen (Karten, Blätter, Prospekte, Kataloge)
Das Typoplakat
Das Bildplakat
Schildformate, Tafeln und Rahmen
Inserate
Die Zeitschrift
Die Tageszeitung
Die illustrierte Zeitung
Tabellensatz
Das neue Buch

Bibliographie
Verzeichnis der Abbildungen
Register

typ. tschichold

Das Buch enthält über 125 Abbildungen, von
denen etwa ein Viertel **zweifarbig** gedruckt ist,
und umfaßt gegen **200** Seiten auf gutem Kunst-
druckpapier. Es erscheint im Format DIN A5 (148×
210 mm) und ist biegsam in Ganzleinen gebunden.

Preis bei Vorbestellung bis 1. Juni 1928: **5.**00 RM
durch den Buchhandel nur zum Preise von **6.**50 RM

Bestellschein umstehend ■▶

The Practice of Typography were really about conventional composing-room practice and were designed for the trade, since professional typographers did not then exist. Stanley Morison's *First Principles of Typography* – in any case, a short article, not a book – first appeared two years later, in *The Fleuron* No.7 in 1930. D. B. Updike's *In the Day's Work*, 1924, although full of typographic wisdom, is far from being a systematic statement of design principles. Francis Meynell's *Typography*, 1923, beautifully designed and produced, was basically an elaborate advertisement of Meynell's Pelican Press. Paul Renner's *Typografie als Kunst* ('Typography as an Art'), 1922, was very good, and Tschichold remembers studying it eagerly. It was an excellent introduction to design and typography, with some rules, and an 'ABC of Typography', but it was entirely limited to books, and was, incidentally, set in black-letter. Joseph Thorp's *Printing for Business*, 1919, deserves mention here as perhaps the earliest attempt to provide a description of printing practice in non-technical language, with examples and illustrations of good design, but it was addressed to printers' customers rather than to typographers; and although it embraced all fields of printing, not books alone, it was extremely limited in scope and outlook.

Tschichold was himself already a master designer. *Die neue Typographie* is still today, nearly fifty years later, a distinguished example of book production both in look and feel. It was produced in A5 format, bound in limp fine black cloth, lettered on the spine in silver; set entirely in sans serif, with a dramatic solid black frontispiece facing the title-page that has now been illustrated in many articles and books on book design. Today, in contrast to much of the avant-garde typography of that time, it looks elegant rather than brutal because Tschichold had in fact already assimilated the traditional principles of typographic design and was putting them into practice, although in an unconventional way.

The text and illustrations provided a masterly survey of the art of typography; but it was the vision of a young man, who had at last seen the light himself, was convinced that his beliefs were the only truth, and firmly believed that the sooner they were recognized by everyone else the better and fuller life would be. Tschichold was proclaiming the birth of a new period of European culture and proclaiming it passionately. To remember the times and country in which he lived is to understand and sympathize with his passion, and that of the many other young artists in all fields of creativity who also saw hope only in what was new.

A strain of socialist idealism runs through *Die neue Typographie*, just as it did in the life and work of William Morris. Both men saw that design is not something abstract but has to be an expression of men's lives. Morris saw, only too clearly, the horrible effects of factories and machines on men's lives and turned his back

JAN TSCHICHOLD

DIE NEUE TYPOGRAPHIE

EIN HANDBUCH FÜR ZEITGEMÄSS SCHAFFENDE

BERLIN **1928**
VERLAG DES BILDUNGSVERBANDES DER DEUTSCHEN BUCHDRUCKER

Title-page double spread of *Die neue Typographie*, Berlin, 1928. Reduced. The subtitle would read in modern English 'A handbook for modern designers'.

on the machine. Tschichold saw factory production as making possible a new era of human happiness, and wrote ecstatically of 'the works of today, untainted by the past, primary shapes which identify the aspect of our time: Car Aeroplane Telephone Radio Neon New York! These objects, designed without reference to the aesthetics of the past, have been created by a new kind of man: THE ENGINEER!' He also several times decried the 'selfish individualism' of the individual artist, and proclaimed the virtues of man-produced objects like electric light bulbs. From this, he went on to say that works of art can be mass-produced; he was writing at the time of the geometrical compositions of

Beziehungen nachzuweisen und seine Konsequenzen darzulegen, Klarheit über die Elemente der Typographie und die Forderung zeitgemäßer typographischer Gestaltung zu schaffen, ist Gegenstand dieses Buchs. Der Zusammenhang der Typographie mit allen anderen Gestaltungsgebieten, vor allem der Architektur, hat in allen bedeutenden Zeiten bestanden. Heute erleben wir die Geburt einer neuen, großartigen Baukunst, die unserer Zeit das Gepräge geben wird. Wer einmal die tiefe innere Ähnlichkeit der Typographie mit der Baukunst erkannt und die Neue Architektur ihrem Wesen nach begreifen gelernt hat, für den kann kein Zweifel mehr daran sein, daß die Zukunft der Neuen und nicht der alten Typographie gehören wird.

Und es ist unmöglich, daß etwa, wie manche meinen, auch in Zukunft beide Typographien wie noch heute weiter nebeneinander bestehen. Der kommende große Stil wäre keiner, wenn neben der zeitgemäßen noch die Renaissanceform auf irgendwelchen Gebieten, sei es Buchdruck oder Architektur, weiter existierte. Der Romantismus der vergehenden Generation, so verständlich er ist, hat noch nie einen neuen Stil verhindert. So wie es heute absurd ist, Villen wie Rokokoschlösser oder wie gotische Burgen zu bauen wie vor vierzig Jahren, wird man morgen diejenigen belächeln, die die alte Typographie noch weiter zu erhalten trachten.

In dem Kampfe zwischen dem Alten und dem Neuen handelt es sich nicht um die Erschaffung einer neuen Form um ihrer selbst willen. Aber die neuen Bedürfnisse und Inhalte schaffen sich selbst eine auch äußerlich veränderte Gestalt. Und so wenig man diese neuen Bedürfnisse hinwegdisputieren kann, so wenig ist es möglich, die Notwendigkeit einer wirklich zeitgemäßen Typographie zu bestreiten.

Darum hat der Buchdrucker heute die Pflicht, sich um diese Fragen zu bemühen. Einige sind mit Energie und Elan schöpferisch vorangegangen. für die anderen aber gilt es noch fast

ALLES !
zu tun ❗

DIE ALTE TYPOGRAPHIE (1450—1914)

Während die Geschichte der Typographie von der Erfindung bis etwa zur Mitte des vorigen Jahrhunderts eine fortlaufende, ruhige Entwicklungskurve zeigt, bietet die Entwicklung seit dieser Zeit das Bild ruckweiser, unorganischer Störungen, einander durchkreuzender Bewegungen, die Tatsachen neuer technischer Erfindungen, die auf die Entwicklung bestimmend einwirken.

Die Typographie der ersten Epoche (1440—1850) beschränkt sich fast ausschließlich auf das Buch. Die Gestaltung der daneben auftauchenden Flugzettel und der wenigen Zeitungen entspricht der der Buchseite. Bestimmendes Element, besonders seit dem Anfang des 16. Jahrhunderts, ist die Type. Die übrigen Teile des Buches erscheinen sekundär, sie sind angefügt, schmückend, nicht Wesensbestandteil. Die Buchgestalt als Ganzes wird im Laufe der Jahrhunderte zwar variiert, aber nicht entscheidend gewandelt. Gutenberg, der nichts anderes im Sinne hatte, als die damalige Buchform — die Handschrift — zu imitieren, entwickelte seine Typen aus der damaligen Buchschrift, der gotischen Minuskel. Sie, die man heute gern religiösen und anderen feierlichen Inhalten vorbehält, diente zu ihrer Zeit zur Niederschrift oder zum Druck a l l e r vorkommenden, auch profaner, Texte. Der Erfinder wählte mit der gotischen Minuskel, der „Textur", eine Schrift zum Vorbild, die für Inhalte von Bedeutung, d. h. für solche Bücher verwendet wurde, deren Inhalt den Horizont nur aktuellen Interesses überschritt. Neben dieser gotischen Minuskel war im täglichen Leben für aktuelle Schriften, Urkunden und kurze Niederschriften die gotische Kursive (in Frankreich Bâtarde genannt) in Gebrauch, die später Schoeffer zur Ausgangsform der von ihm zuerst benutzten Schwabacher machte. Mit diesen zwei Schriftarbeiten begnügte sich das Zeitalter zwischen der Erfindung und dem Beginn des 16. Jahrhunderts. Von den Variationen der Gotisch und der Schwabacher, die mit den Schriften Gutenbergs und Schoeffers die allgemeine Linienführung gemein haben, dürfen wir bei dieser historischen Betrachtung ebenso absehen, wie von den Formen der Antiquatype vor 1500.

Die Buchform als Ganzes gleicht zu dieser Zeit fast vollkommen der Form des geschriebenen spätgotischen Kodex. Sein Reichtum an bemalten, goldgehöhten großen und farbigen kleinen Initialen, die Rubrikatur, die Randleisten der Anfangsseiten werden in das gedruckte Buch übernommen. Ursprünglich mit der Hand eingefügt, werden diese schmückenden Teile bald in Holz geschnitten und mit g e d r u c k t, bei kostbareren Ausführungen eines Buches nachträglich koloriert. Der Satz in zwei Kolumnen überwiegt. Die Titel zeigen eine asymmetrische, von Logik nicht übermäßig belastete Aufteilung. Selten, daß axiale Gliederungen erscheinen — sie bleiben auf Italien beschränkt. Die Harmonie von Text, Initialen und Titelei wird von

14   15

Double-spread from *Die neue Typographie*, 1928. Reduced.

Mondrian and the photographic works of El Lissitzky and Man Ray. He was in fact much influenced by the work of the Russians, especially El Lissitzky. He hoped, as so many other intelligent and idealistic people then did, that the Russian revolution might offer a solution to some of the world's problems. He did not join the Communist Party, and did not spend any time in purely political activities, but for a few years he signed his work 'Ivan (or Iwan) Tschichold'.

Reading *Die neue Typographie* today, we can see that some of the ideas expressed are extremely naïve, and some are quite mistaken. Tschichold later regretted them

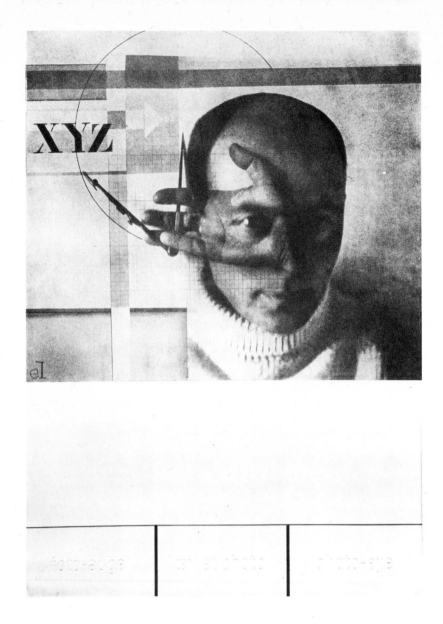

Cover of *foto-auge*, 1929. A collection of 76 contemporary photographs edited by Tschichold and Franz Roh. Original in black with blind embossed lettering at foot.

and the dogmatic tones in which the whole book was written: but his basic message was sound, and it needed saying. He was insisting on simplicity and purity in design, on the necessity of fitting design to modern printing methods (i.e. 'functionalism') and of making design 'modern', in harmony with the new modern world being created round us. It was urgently necessary to clear away the rubbish of the past, and any study of average German printing in the 1920s, especially advertisement pages in newspapers and magazines, will show how necessary and indeed urgent the task was: half measures would have been no good. So symmetry in layout had to go: asymmetry was more functional (in

Jan Tschichold

EINE STUNDE DRUCKGESTALTUNG

Grundbegriffe der Neuen Typografie in Bildbeispielen
für Setzer, Werbefachleute, Drucksachenverbraucher und Bibliofilen

Akademischer Verlag Dr. Fritz Wedekind & Co.   Stuttgart   **1930**

Title spread from *Eine Stunde Druckgestaltung,* 1930.

some senses in typographical design it actually is, because it is more flexible, and arguably easier for machine compositors) and asymmetry permitted subtle rhythms and tensions which complemented those being explored by the modern abstract painters and sculptors like Mondrian, El Lissitzky, Kandinsky and Malevich. Coupled with this was the conviction that the only type-face capable of expressing the new age was sans serif: it was the bare bones of lettering, the primal, elementary letter-shapes, the only true visual expression of the twentieth century. True or not, this was all good and useful to say at the time, and it had to be said with all the apostolic fervour that Tschichold could command

because otherwise it would not have been listened to. As it happened,
Tschichold's elegant design and comprehensive account of the new typography
and its important place at the heart of modern art and design produced an
electrifying effect. The book was discussed everywhere, arousing occasionally as
passionate opposition as support, but the trend of typographic design on the
Continent was changed from that day on. Tschichold had given to the young, and
to those with eyes to see, a new gospel, an ideal in which they could believe, a
policy which was clear-cut, revolutionary, dynamic and drastic. However much
we notice and analyse its shortcomings today, we must think of what its impact
must have been on its readers (mostly in Germany and Switzerland, for it was not,
and still has not been, published in translation in any other language) in 1928 and
the following years. It was a seminal work; it dealt explicitly and directly with
the actual problems that had to be faced every day in every printing works, large
and small, all over Europe.

Jan Tschichold: **Schriftschreiben für Setzer**

Double spread from *Schriftschreiben für Setzer*.

24 **Antiqua** (8)

Die Antiqua, eine Mischung der Kapitalformen mit der Karlingischen Minuskel, versieht die Minuskelformen mit gleichen oder ähnlichen Schraffen wie die Versalien, um den stilistischen Zwiespalt zwischen Versalien und ›Gemeinen‹ zu mindern. Die Antiqua ist eine Erfindung der Renaissance und wird von den Schreibern gegen Ende des 15. Jahrhunderts aus der wieder aufgenommenen Karlingischen Minuskel entwickelt. Sie bildet die Vorlage für die ersten reinen Antiquatypen, für die Mediävalantiqua (siehe das geschichtliche Beispiel Seite 26).

Die Grundformen der Versalien sind die unserer ›Rustika‹ (Seite 11), die der Gemeinen jene der ›Lateinischen Minuskel‹ (Seite 13) Zunächst nehmen wir eine Rundschriftfeder 2¹/₂ (—To 62¹/₂) und schreiben damit die n-Größe auf 2 Kästchen (2 Cicero). Die Oberlängen sind 1¹/₂ Kästchen (3 Nonpareille) höher, die Unterlängen fast ebensoviel länger. Später kann man mit schmäleren Federn kleiner schreiben. Immer aber soll die Antiqua zart, der Raum zwischen den Zeilen groß bleiben. Wir können gleich mit Tinte schreiben. Die Schraffen etwa des I sind straff waagerecht und kurz zu halten. Der schräge Ansatz, wie er etwa beim i oben und beim h oben erscheint wird mit einem schrägen Abstrich nach links begonnen. Dann schreibt man, ohne abzusetzen, einen schrägen hohlen Bogen nach rechts, setzt jetzt ab und schreibt von oben her den Senkrechten. Vergleiche das Beispiel nebenan. Die Antiqua setzt große Sorgfalt beim Schreiben voraus. Sie soll exakt, aber nicht gezwungen, sondern flüssig wirken. Alle Bogen (bei n, m, h, u, c, d, a, g, p, r, s, f, ff, ß, j, U, C, G, S, J) müssen,

sehr flach geschrieben werden; hohe Bogen würden optische Flecken ergeben und den Lauf der Zeile stören.

Die Abstriche bei u, d und a sind kleine, die des l und t dagegen große Bogen.

Die Versalien müssen wie in allen Schriften ein wenig kleiner geschrieben werden als die Oberlängen der Gemeinen. Die Ziffern gleichen denen der lateinischen Minuskel von Seite 13; nur die ı erhält unten eine Schraffe.

Durch leichte Schrägstellung und Engerführung läßt sich aus unserer Antiqua unschwer eine passende Kursiv entwickeln. Das Wort ›und‹ der letzten Zeile der gegenüberstehenden Vorschrift zeigt ein Beispiel. Man übe aber vorher die einfache Kursiv von Seite 31.

Das historische Beispiel auf Seite 26 gibt eine schön geschriebene Buchseite wieder aus der Zeit, als man die karlingische Minuskel zu neuem Leben erweckte. Sie zeigt besonders edle Verhältnisse des Zeilenzwischenraums und der Ränder.

So schreibt man den Kopf oben bei i und h:

25

inmhulocdqeapbrsg ff ff tt ttt ·
vwxyjzkß . , : ; - ! ? 1500
ILHEFTUOQCGDSJJPB
RKVWAXZYNM
Antiqua besteht
aus Versalien *und* Gemeinen

Single-alphabet type designed by Tschichold,
1929. Phonetic version is shown opposite.

für den neuen menschen existiert
nur das gleichgewicht zwischen
natur und geist   zu jedem zeit-
punkt der vergangenheit waren
alle variationen des alten ›neu‹·
aber es war nicht ›das‹ neue· wir

It was not included in the *Printing and the Mind of Man* Exhibition in London
in 1963, in which the sole example of the 'new typography' was Mayakovsky's
book of poems *Dlya golosa* ('For the Voice'), Berlin 1923, designed by El
Lissitzky, referred to and illustrated in *Die neue Typographie*; an ingenious experiment,
which certainly impressed Tschichold, but not one capable of bearing fruit to
nourish those who had to perform the daily tasks of the printing trade.

Die neue Typographie was, of course, almost completely ignored in England in the
years immediately following its publication – understandably, since it was
written in German. But there was some awareness of Tschichold's work. In July
1930, the monthly magazine *Commercial Art* (published by *The Studio*)
published an extremely well illustrated nineteen-page article 'New Life in Print'
by Tschichold, in which he explained what the 'New Typography' was all about.
The slow progress in England at that time of modern art, modern architecture
and modern typography is now only too evident; but in any case, Tschichold
could not then compete with the dominance of Stanley Morison, who in 1930
completed (in his own words) 'the 1500 pages in which *The Fleuron* has discussed
typography – that admittedly minor technicality of civilized life . . .' without
including, as far as I can discover, any reference at all to 'modern typography'
beyond the lofty instructions in the last paragraph but one of the last article
in the last *Fleuron*: 'The apostles of the "machine-age" will be wise to address their
disciples in a standard old face – they can flourish their concrete banner in sans
serif on title-pages and perhaps in a running headline.' The twenty-six-page index
to the seven volumes of *The Fleuron* contains no reference to Tschichold, to the
Bauhaus or anyone connected with it (but to many other contemporary
European printers), to anything avant-garde or to photography. Although not

für den noien menſen eksistirt nur das glaihgeviht tsviſen natur unt gaist· tsu jedem tsaitpunkt der fergazenhait varen ale variatsjonen des alten ›noi‹· aber es var niht ›das‹ noie· vir dürfen niht

successful in spelling his name, Morison had in fact heard of and admired Tschichold *as a calligrapher* in 1927 and had defended him when a capitalist pen-manufacturer had described Tschichold as communist – as related in an amusing letter to Walter Lewis quoted by Nicolas Barker in *Stanley Morison*, 1972, p.213. Tschichold's first opportunity to visit and work in Britain, given him by Lund Humphries in 1935, is described in the next chapter.

After *Die neue Typographie*, Tschichold published *foto-auge* (photo-eye), a ninety-six-page booklet of modern photographs, edited by himself and Franz Roh, 1929; *Eine Stunde Druckgestaltung* (An hour of print design), 1930, a 100-page booklet in A4 size with an elegant cover in ribbed silver paper printed in red and black, consisting mostly of photographs reproduced in half-tone, of all kinds of printed matter, advertisements, posters, letter-heads, newspapers, magazines and books, showing examples of the bad old design and the good new, with explanations; *Schriftschreiben für Setzer* (Lettering for Compositors), 1931, a landscape A5 booklet of thirty-two pages on coated paper, in light blue paper covers, teaching compositors and typographers how to draw the type-faces they use in layouts; and *Typographische Entwurfstechnik* (The Technique of Drawing Layouts), 1932, an A4 booklet of twenty-four pages on coated paper, in bright yellow paper covers, prescribing that designers and compositors should make their layouts an exact representation of the finished job, and showing them how; it also provides a very good basic introduction to typographic design.

foto-auge and *Fototek I*, the first in a series of photography studies designed and co-edited by Tschichold, are both good examples of his work in book design at this time, and would look distinguished in any company.

Cover of *Typografische Entwurfstechnik*, 1932. The cover, which was originally in A4 size, printed in black on yellow paper, demonstrates the range of DIN A paper sizes.

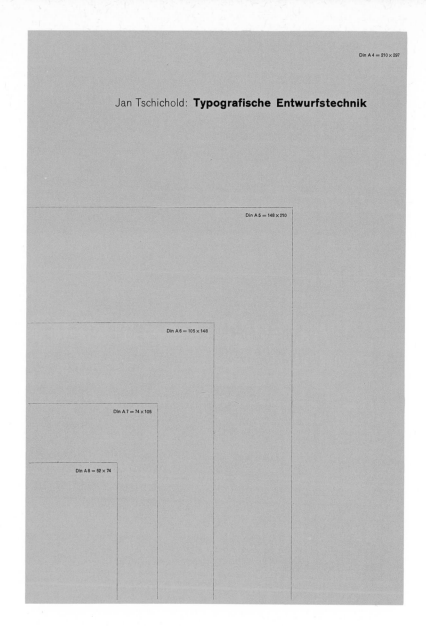

Jan Tschichold: **Typografische Entwurfstechnik**

Din A 4 = 210 × 297

Din A 5 = 148 × 210

Din A 6 = 105 × 148

Din A 7 = 74 × 105

Din A 8 = 52 × 74

foto-auge (in which no capitals were used, a device which Tschichold abandoned by about 1930) was an important work, one of the earliest anthologies of the new photography. It was a paperback in A4 size. Its cover consisted of El Lissitzky's famous self-portrait, printed (to bleed) from a half-tone on a smooth cartridge, with the title (in German, French and English) embossed in blind along the foot, inside black rules (p.38). The flat spine carried the titles reversed out of a red block with 'roh+tschichold' overprinted in black. Inside, Roh's text was printed in German, French and English (poorly translated and mis-spelled), set in Bodoni, and Bodoni Bold, without caps, using a bold sans serif for display lines. The illustrations included straight photographs, air photos, medical photos,

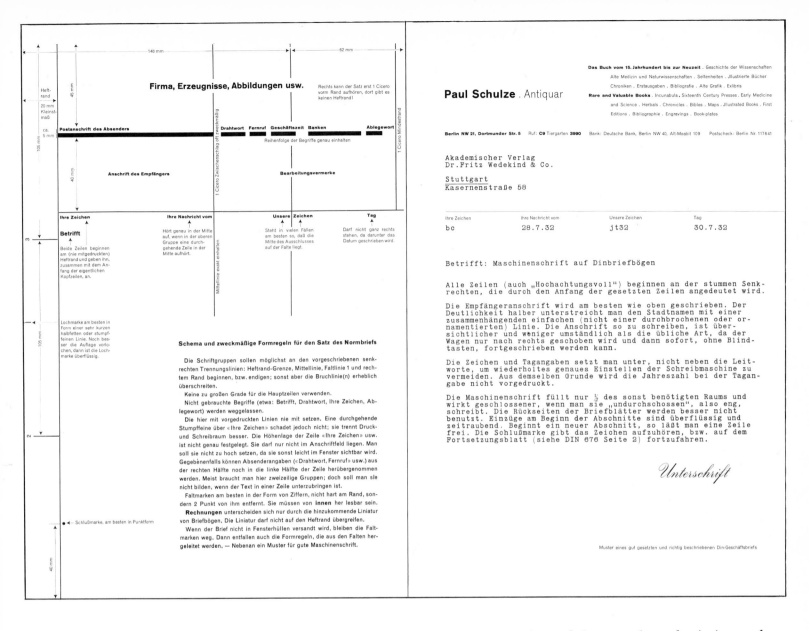

Double spread from *Typografische Entwurfstechnik*, 1932, demonstrating the grid on which a business letter-heading should be designed.

photograms, photo-montage, combinations of photography and painting, and photographic posters, all printed from half-tone blocks on matt coated paper. The book was printed on one side of the paper only; the pages were folded concertina-fashion like a Japanese book, and wire-stabbed.

Fototek I was the first part of a new series on modern photography, edited by Franz Roh and designed by Tschichold, the subject being Laszlo Moholy-Nagy. The advertisement at the back of the book for forthcoming titles in the series announces as the fourth title a work on photo-montage by Tschichold, which never appeared. *Fototek* was produced in the size of 250 × 175 mm, half-way

between A5 and A4, and in the same proportions. Tschichold would at that time probably have repudiated the suggestion that *foto-auge* and *Fototek* showed his 'style', since in *Die neue Typographie* he inveighs against individualism and personal styles, and would have claimed that he was practising merely a logical and international style. So he was, but whatever style or rules one follows there is always a difference between the work of the creative designer and the competent workman. All Tschichold's work had a quality that makes it distinctive and distinguished, never boring. There is a meticulous sense of space and positioning but also a sense of surprise in an unexpected material, a colour combination, a piece of visual playfulness, as in the slanting of the title type on the cover of *Fototek I* which echoes the diagonal in the photograph above.

L. Moholy-Nagy

60 Fotos	herausgegeben von Franz Roh
60 photos	edited by Franz Roh
60 photographies	publiées par Franz Roh

Klinkhardt & Biermann   Verlag - Publishers - Editeurs   Berlin W 10

He was refining his typographic style, both in the more subtle construction of complicated layouts and in the cleverer use of different weights of type in the same size. The order form for *Die neue Typographie* (p.34) uses six different sizes of type; the Book Club circular of 1932 on p.51 has only three. The order form is a powerful layout, but the circular is more graceful. (This was for a publisher in Berlin for whom Tschichold had wholly designed a large number of books between 1929 and 1933.)

In these few years Tschichold had succeeded in formulating a completely new philosophy of typographic design, which held great promise for the future. It was abruptly threatened by the advent of the Third Reich.

Four film posters designed by Tschichold for
Phoebus Palast, Munich.
'Casanova': 1927. White background above, light
blue below. Circular photo in violet-grey,
headline in vermilion.
'Die Sünde am Kinde': 1927. Black and blue on
pink.
'Kiki': 1927. Background yellow, type in black
and brown.
'Die Hose': 1927. Red and black on white.

Tschichold's film posters and the whole New Typography movement were
turned into a political issue. The Nazis soon let it be known that they intended to
eradicate the 'New Typography' together with the modern movement in painting,
with which it was integrally linked. The Nazis wanted their propaganda printed
in black-letter. The 'modern movement' was 'decadent' and labelled 'Kultur-
Bolschevismus'.

In Munich at the beginning of 1933, it was not believed that things would go
Hitler's way in Bavaria. Tschichold was on a lecture trip in Stuttgart and
Donaueschingen, when in early March 1933 armed Nazis entered his Munich flat
on the excuse of a house-to-house search. He and his wife were then arrested,

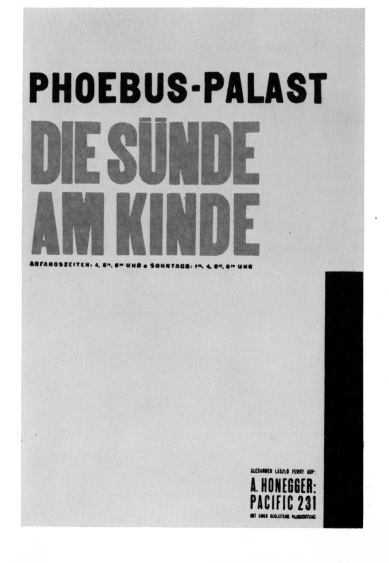

and placed in 'protective custody', she for only a few days, he for six weeks. In prison, Tschichold learned that his teaching contract had been cancelled – at the Nazis' request.

Tschichold saw that Germany was sliding into the abyss, and with a wife and four-year-old son to think of, decided on emigration. Thanks to the intervention of the then Director of the Basle School of Arts and Crafts, Dr Hermann Kienzle, he was offered a small retainer by a Basle publishing and printing firm, Benno Schwabe, and the security of some hours teaching in the School. On 1 August 1933, he was a free man in Riehen, near Basle.

NORMA TALMADGE
IN **KiKi**

PHOEBUS PALACE

SHOWING AT . . . 400 615 830
SUNDAYS . . . 145 400 615 830

Book-jacket designed by Tschichold, 1931.
Actual size. Original in black and red on light green.

Thomas Morus	**16.** Jahrhundert
Bellamy	**19.** Jahrhundert
Illing	**20.** Jahrhundert

Illing

**uto-
polis**

Werner Illing

utopolis

Phantastischer Zukunftsroman

„Ein Zukunftsgemälde einer freien Gemeinschaft Utopien mit der Hauptstadt Utopolis. Von erfinderischer Phantasie mit allen technisch-mechanischen Fortschrittsmöglichkeiten ausgestattet • In vielem ist das Buch Gegenwartssatire am Stoff einer imaginär erschauten Zukunft. Illing hat Phantasie, einen einfachen, bildhaft genauen, unprätentiösen Stil und als Bestes eine gute, tatwillige Gesinnung."   Die Literatur.

In Ganzleinen gebunden 4.30 RM

Leaflet for a publisher, designed by Tschichold, 1932. Reduced. Original in black on pink paper.

Verlag Der Bücherkreis GmbH   Berlin SW 61

An unsere Zahlstellenleiter, Werber und Freunde!

In früheren Jahren ist öfter über die Ausstattung unserer Werke geklagt worden. In den letzten beiden Jahren haben wir versucht, diesen Beschwerden nachzugehen und die Mängel abzustellen. Als Mitarbeiter zogen wir einen der bekanntesten neuzeitlichen Buchkünstler, nämlich **Jan Tschichold,** München, heran und übertrugen ihm die gesamte typographische Ausstattung unserer Verlagswerke.
Wir können heute mit Befriedigung feststellen, daß die Beschwerden über die Ausstattung so gut wie verstummt sind. Aus den Kreisen unserer Mitglieder und der Zahlstellenleiter erhielten wir dagegen vielfach lobende Äußerungen. Zu der besseren graphischen Ausstattung kam die Verbesserung der stofflichen Qualität. Vorzügliches Papier, sorgfältige Buchbinderarbeit und solider, kräftiger Einband sind die Kennzeichen unserer Bände. Neuerdings erhalten unsere Bücher auch stets eine Buchhülle, die von den Vertriebsstellen und den Lesern sehr geschätzt wird.
In einer ganzen Anzahl von **graphischen Fachausstellungen des In- und Auslandes** sind unsere Bücher und Werbedrucksachen ausgestellt worden. Unsere von Tschichold betreuten Arbeiten haben dabei in der Kritik Auszeichnung und Lob gefunden. **Viele Fachzeitschriften der graphischen Gewerbe** haben unsere Bücher besprochen und die Ausstattung ohne Ausnahme gelobt. Die Zeitschrift **„Der moderne Buchdrucker"** z. B. brachte in Heft 1/2, Frühjahr 1932, eine empfehlende Wiedergabe zweier Text-Seiten aus Wöhrles „Jan Hus" in einem Artikel „Gedanken zu einer Ausstellung schöner, auf der Linotype gesetzter Bücher". Der 25. Jubiläumsjahrgang von **„Klimschs Jahrbuch der graphischen Künste 1932"** brachte je vier Abbildungen auf vier Seiten von der Ausstattung und dem Satz unserer Verlagswerke Wendlers „Laubenkolonie Erdenglück" und Mänchen-Helfens „Tuwa-Buch", was eine besondere Anerkennung unserer Arbeit bedeutet.

Nachfolgend geben wir Ihnen **gekürzte** Ausführungen einiger Fachblätter bekannt.

„Graphische Jahrbücher", Monatsschrift für das gesamte graphische Gewerbe:
„ . . . Mänchens Reisebericht, dem übrigens viele prächtige photographische Abbildungen beigegeben sind, bietet also nach den verschiedensten Richtungen hin eine Fülle des Interessanten. Es gibt nicht allzuviele Bücher, denen das gegeben ist, und darum kann es nicht dringend genug empfohlen werden."

Dieselbe Zeitschrift in einem anderen Heft:
„ . . . Eines der interessantesten Bücher (Grisars „Europa-Buch") liegt vor uns. Die Bilder selbst sind von einer bezwingenden Natürlichkeit. Sie sind auf ein Mattpapier gedruckt und dem ganzen Buche systematisch eingegliedert. Das Buch selbst ist typographisch einwandfrei ausgestattet; . . . obwohl wir zugeben müssen, daß man bei der Art der Anordnung der Bilder dieser lapidaren Formensprache durch die Wahl der Grotesk am ehesten gerecht wird. Das Buch ist samt seinen Jllustrationen vorzüglich gedruckt. Der Einband ist besonders wirkungsvoll . . ."

„Jahrbuch des Deutschen Vereins für Buchwesen und Schrifttum" (Dr. Hans H. Bockwitz):
„ . . . Von dieser Reise brachte er eine Menge aufschlußreicher Forschungsergebnisse und eine Anzahl sehr interessanter Photos mit, von denen 28 dem von Jan Tschichold typographisch vorzüglich gestalteten Buche beigegeben sind . . ."

„Zeitschrift für Bücherfreunde", Leipzig (Professor Georg Witkowski):
„ . . . Der von Jan Tschichold entworfene Einband und der Titel verdienen ein besonderes Lob . . ."

Book-jacket designed by Tschichold, 1931.
Reduced. Original in black and red.

Mensch unterm Hammer

Roman von Josef Lenhard

Die sonderbare Geschichte des sonderbaren Proleten
Kilian Narr aus der katholischen bayerischen Pfalz. Un-
bändiger Freiheits- und Wissensdrang bringt ihn unauf-
hörlich in Widerstreit mit allen möglichen Obrigkeiten.
Dieser Kilian Narr ist zur guten Hälfte Josef Lenhard selbst,
der in diesen seinem Erstlingsroman voll bittern Humors
Gericht über sich selbst hält.   In Ganzleinen 4.30 RM

Business card for Edith Tschichold, Munich,
1927.

edith tschichold

planegg bei münchen hofmarckstrasse 39

Design for a poster, 1932, not used. Reduced.
Original in black and yellow.

FESTIVALS of the Bavarian State Theatres · **Munich**

July 18th to August 28th, 1932

Prince Regent Theatre: **Richard Wagner**
Residence Theatre: **W.A.Mozart**

followed by a Richard **Strauss** and Hans **Pfitzner** Week in the Prince Regent Theatre

Wagner-Mozart

Monday	July 18	Die Meistersinger
Wednesday	July 20	Das Rheingold
Thursday	July 21	Figaros Hochzeit
Friday	July 22	Die Walküre
Saturday	July 23	Die Zauberflöte
Sunday	July 24	Siegfried
Tuesday	July 26	Götterdämmerung
Wednesday	July 27	Don Giovanni

Monday	July 28	Die Meistersinger
Wednesday	July 29	Das Rheingold
Thursday	July 30	Figaros Hochzeit
Friday	July 31	Die Walküre
Saturday	Aug 3	Die Zauberflöte
Sunday	Aug 4	Siegfried
Tuesday	Aug 5	Götterdämmerung
Wednesday	Aug 6	Don Giovanni

Monday	Aug 7	Die Meistersinger
Wednesday	Aug 8	Das Rheingold
Thursday	Aug 9	Figaros Hochzeit
Friday	Aug 11	Die Walküre
Saturday	Aug 12	Die Zauberflöte
Sunday	Aug 13	Siegfried
Tuesday	Aug 14	Götterdämmerung
Wednesday	Aug 15	Don Giovanni

Monday	Aug 16	Die Meistersinger
Wednesday	Aug 18	Das Rheingold
Thursday	Aug 19	Figaros Hochzeit
Friday	Aug 20	Die Walküre
Saturday	Aug 21	Die Zauberflöte
Sunday	Aug 22	Siegfried

Richard Strauss

Monday	Aug 23	Der Rosenkavalier
Wednesday	Aug 24	Salome

Hans Pfitzner

Saturday	Aug 27	Palestrina
Sunday	Aug 28	Der arme Heinrich

Prices of admission
to Wagner Performances   RM 23.50 18.– ...
to Mozart Performances   RM 33.50 18.– 13.50 7.30
to Strauss-Pfitzner Performances RM 14.50 9.– 4.50

→ Seats may be booked
at the Amtliches Bayrisches Reiseburo, 16 Promenadeplatz,
Munich, or at the Tageskasse der Staatstheater, Max Joseph
Platz Munich

Paul Graupe Berlin W 9 Bellevuestrasse 7

Am 17. und 18. Oktober 1932 : **Auktion 105**

Bücher	Die grafische Sammlung	Sammlung
des 15. bis 20. Jahrhunderts	Rudolf Tewes	Paul Ephraim, Berlin
Inkunabeln	Französische Meister	Gemälde
Holzschnittbücher	des 19. und 20. Jahrhunderts:	Handzeichnungen
Erstausgaben	Daumier, Degas, Manet,	neuerer deutscher Meister
Luxus- und Pressendrucke	Picasso, Renoir	
Kunstliteratur	Eine umfassende	
	Toulouse-Lautrec-Sammlung	

Illustrierter Katalog auf Wunsch

After Tschichold's departure, typography in Germany remained as sterile and wretched as it had been in the pre-1925 period. The large advertisements of big firms, still mostly drawn by hand, and still unbelievably tasteless, showed that nothing had been learned. Book design remained static, as was to be expected under the Nazi régime, which could not tolerate what it could not understand.

An officially sponsored exhibition of German book production was held in London in 1937 and was reviewed in *Typography* 3 of Summer 1937. It was noted there that ordinary commercial book production was not represented, except for 'the charming collection of small and inexpensive Insel-Verlag productions' (forerunners of the King Penguins, and then costing the equivalent of about one shilling). If it had been, it would not have compared very favourably, from the design point of view, with the best British 'ordinary books' of the same period, e.g. the normal books from Gollancz, Cape, Chatto, Faber, or the Oxford and Cambridge University Presses. The exhibition concentrated on German private press books, and *Typography*'s reviewer commented: 'The historically correct margins, the carefully handset types, the general disposition of the material assured one that the English private pressmen had not laboured in vain.' These were the works of Tiemann (Janus-Presse), Ehmcke (Rupprecht-

Presse), Wiegand (Bremer-Presse) and Kleukens (Ernst-Ludwig and Kleukens-Presse). One of the strongest influences on German printing design at the time was Rudolf Koch, whose devotion to traditional Gothic letter forms was favoured by the authorities and who did not live long enough to discern the true nature of the Nazis. Of Koch's best pupils, Fritz Kredel and Warren Chappell went to America, and Berthold Wolpe came to England. Books associated with these designers, or with illustrations by Willi Harwerth or Alfred Mahlau, are among the pleasantest 'ordinary' books which appeared in Germany before 1939: they were usually set in black-letter. Most of the creative brains in German publishing under Hitler either fled from Germany and enriched other countries, principally England, America and Switzerland, or did not survive.

Transito. Alphabet designed by Tschichold for Lettergieterij Amsterdam, 1931.

Le Capital FONDERIE

Saskia. Alphabet designed by Tschichold for Schelter und Giesecke, Leipzig, 1931.

SASKIA

frohe Farben in das sonnige Bild des Sommers

zu tragen, und alle modischen Pastelltöne

finden die anderen, die für ihre Erscheinung

eine ruhigere Note lieben. Kurz- oder lang-

ärmelige Jäckchen werden zu diesen duftigen

55

Chapter 4   In Switzerland 1933-46

Tschichold was admitted into Switzerland as a recognized specialist and, as such, was granted a limited work permit. The struggle to start a new life was, at first, hard and bitter. Every penny had to be counted. Things would have been much worse but for a small income he still received for work he had done in Munich for the photo-composition firm of Uhertype. He had designed about ten faces for Uhertype early in 1933, and was well paid for them, but it seems that the management or policy of the firm changed, they were never used, and have since been lost. This work was no longer open to him. The effects of the collapse of Wall Street on Black Friday, 24 October 1929, were as severe in Switzerland as in Germany – where it had been one of the factors leading to the rise of Hitler. Even in Switzerland there was still much unemployment.

The average quality of Swiss typography was then even lower than in Germany. Tschichold realized the urgent necessity of establishing a set of house rules to be used in his new place of employment, Benno Schwabe, to try to overcome the centuries-old tradition of bad design which still prevailed. The first three of his new rules may be quoted here:

1. All display lines in jobbing and advertising work, and the text in books and other higher quality work, must be spaced with *thick* spaces. Especially in hand composition, optically even word spacing is to be aimed at, especially after punctuation and in the change between roman and italic.
2. After *full points*, use only the normal word space of the line. Only in long lines may a larger space be used. In long lines, a space in front of commas and hyphens may also be used. Between a word and its parenthesis mark, a space should be inserted, except after a full point and in very short lines.
3. *Display lines* and lines on a title-page should be set without full points.

Cover of booklet for the photo-composition firm of Uhertype, designed by Tschichold, 1934. Reduced. Original in red and black.

UHERTYPE CO. LTD. Glaris (Switzerland), Office: Zurich, 15 Talstrasse

UHERTYPE

Photo-Composing technic

for Job-Work in Offset, Photogravure and Book-Printing

Cover for *Begegnungen*, 1933. Original in
black and yellow.

Gotthard Jedlicka: **Begegnungen**

Gotthard Jedlicka

Begegnungen

Pascin
Liebermann
Maillol
Despiau
Matisse
Braque
Derain
Picasso
Ensor

These are merely three out of fourteen house rules. Anyone who thought it necessary to mention such rules today would be laughed at. The other rules were all equally elementary. They were badly needed and difficult to enforce.

Most of Tschichold's new work was now the designing of books for various Basle publishing houses, mainly Schwabe, Birkhäuser and Holbein.

By 1935, Tschichold had finished his next book, *Typographische Gestaltung* ('Typographic Design'), but the publishers, Benno Schwabe, were not prepared to print if they could not obtain 200 pre-publication orders. However, when they offered their subscription they received, to their great surprise, orders for 1,000 copies and so the book was published in autumn 1935.

It is the same page size as *Die neue Typographie* (A5), bound in blue linen with a paper label on the spine printed in red and black. The text is set in a small size of Bodoni, well leaded (no longer sans serif, which in 1928 had been obligatory for Tschichold) with a bold Egyptian for headings. Most of the book is printed on an uncoated paper, but two sections at the end, illustrated with half-tones, are printed on coated paper. There are several inserts or wrap-rounds of contrasting papers, and illustrations are printed in various colours. The book, less a work of propaganda than *Die neue Typographie*, is a more reasonable and concise statement of the same principles. It is a valuable exposition of the art of typography, much of which is equally applicable to traditional (centred) or asymmetric design. The book was translated into Danish (where it was called *Funktionel Typografi*) and Swedish (*Typografish gestaltning*), and published in Copenhagen and Stockholm in 1937. It was also translated into Dutch, and appeared (as *Typografische vormgeving*) in Amsterdam in 1938. The present writer translated it into English in 1945 but could not find a publisher for it until Messrs Cooper & Beatty, the enterprising type-setters in Toronto, sponsored its publication in 1967 under the title of *Asymmetric Typography*, in conjunction with Reinhold in New York and Faber & Faber in London. This became, in effect, a new edition and, with some changes of illustrations and textual alterations and omissions, was entirely revised and designed by Tschichold. For various reasons, partly the obvious one of expense, the new edition is less visually exciting than the first, but the text, even in translation, remains an important and significant document. No one, to the best of my knowledge, has ever written a more detailed and perceptive account of the principles and practice of typography in English.

In September 1935, Tschichold was invited to lecture to the printers of Copenhagen. In order not to go through Germany and fall into the hands of the Nazis, he had to travel by sea from Ostend to Esbjerg. Later in the same year, he

Jan Tschichold:

Typographische Gestaltung

Benno Schwabe & Co . Basel 1935

Dit boek wil een nieuw typografisch inzicht ingang doen vinden

Typografische vormgeving

Jan Tschichold

● Een nieuwe typografische traditie is de wensch van vele boekdrukkers. Natuurlijk eischen de groote veranderingen in de zet- en druktechniek van de laatste jaren een aangepaste typografische vormgeving. Hierover en over de noodzakelijkheid verantwoord te werken, zooals de oude boekdrukkers, handelt dit boek. De schrijver heeft de vormgeving in den nieuwen typografischen stijl gedurende een reeks van jaren reeds overwegend beïnvloed.

was invited to London by Lund Humphries, the English publishers of this book. At that time, Eric Humphries directed their printing works in Bradford and Eric Gregory their publishing offices in Bedford Square in London. They were one of the most technically advanced and forward-looking printing firms in Europe. It was Edward McKnight Kauffer, the poster designer, who suggested the invitation to Eric Gregory, and a small exhibition of Tschichold's work was held at Bedford Square between 27 November and 14 December, 1935. It was accompanied by an eight-page leaflet, set in Gill Sans, but not designed by Tschichold (it conspicuously lacks his elegance and precision), with a specially-written statement of Tschichold's beliefs about typography translated from the German. The preface, signed by Lund, Humphries & Company, ends with the cautious statement: 'Although we have gladly given an opportunity to Mr Tschichold to hold this Exhibition, we do not therefore imply that we dogmatically abide by his principles of typography. We simply are anxious to let his work, which we believe to be of outstanding merit, speak for itself.' Later, Lund Humphries backed Tschichold more whole-heartedly, commissioned him to redesign their letter-heading (the design was in use from 1936 to 1948, see p.64) and, in 1937, to design the 1938 volume (No.40) of *The Penrose Annual*. Alone among important British printing firms, they have since maintained a consistent policy in the use of modern typography.

On this first visit, Tschichold met Kauffer and Ashley Havinden, then the leading proponents of modern design in London, and also Stanley Morison, in his office at the Fetter Lane headquarters of the Monotype Corporation. He also visited the British Museum and saw for the first time some of its unique collection of old Chinese colour-prints which were to become a lifelong interest.

Although not one of Tschichold's books had yet appeared in an English translation, his work was becoming more and more known in England. In January 1936, Robert Harling wrote an article 'What is this "Functional" Typography? The work of Jan Tschichold' in *Printing*. The summer 1937 issue (No.3) of *Typography* (edited by Robert Harling and published by James Shand of the Shenval Press) contained as its first article six well-illustrated pages on 'Type mixtures' by Tschichold, in which he was able to enunciate several of his principles of design. Also in 1937 he was invited to speak to the Double Crown Club, at its sixty-first dinner, on 'A New Approach to Typography', the president, Walter Lewis, the Printer to Cambridge University, being in the chair. The menu on this page shows just how little of what the 'New Typography' was about had been grasped by the menu designer, or indeed by the Club as a whole.

As testimony to Tschichold's impact on the young, it is perhaps worth adding a personal recollection. I had left school in 1935, aged eighteen, and had spent some

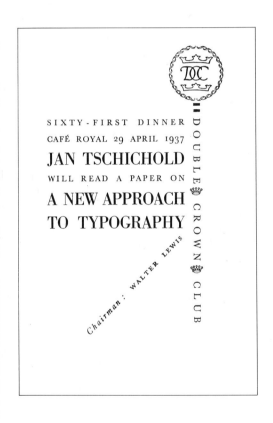

First page of the Double Crown Club Menu on the occasion of Tschichold's talk to the Club, 1937. Designed by a member of the club, it demonstrates how little Tschichold's ideas and those of the modern movement generally were understood in England at that time. Reduced. Original in black, red, blue and gold on cream paper.

months being introduced to printing under the gentle tutelage of Bernard Newdigate at the Shakespeare Head Press in Oxford. Then, thanks to Newdigate's friendship with Anna Simons (Edward Johnston's erstwhile pupil, and translator, in Munich) I went to Germany, on an exchange with a German master printer's son, worked in a printing press in Weimar, and learned some German. My first paid job when I returned home was as book production assistant at *The Studio*, where I worked on Bernard Newdigate's *The Art of the Book*, published by *The Studio* in 1938. It contained eight and a half pages on contemporary German type design and book production, without mentioning the New Typography, but on a later page it did reproduce an opening from *The Penrose Annual* for 1938, designed by Tschichold, with a dry caption by

Letter-heading designed by Tschichold for Lund Humphries, 1935.

lund humphries

Percy Lund Humphries & Co Ltd · The Country Press Bradford   Printers
Publishers
Binders

London Office: 12 Bedford Square, w.c.1
Telephone: Museum 7676
Telegrams: Lund Museum 7676 London

Bradford: Telephone 3408 (two lines)
Telegrams: Typography Bradford

Newdigate, who had no sympathy at all for Tschichold's breaks with tradition, especially his preference for making the inner margins wider than those of the head and fore-edge.

In 1938, aged 21, having in the meantime also worked briefly in an advertising agency, I joined Lund Humphries' printing works in Bradford. On my working desk, I found a sheaf of miscellaneous specimens of Tschichold's work.
I had, by that time, read most of the literature then available in English on typography – there was not much, and it was mostly historical, like
Updike's greatly enjoyed *Printing Types* – but nothing that I can remember had ever gripped my very incipient taste in typography until this. It was perhaps the

Binding design by Tschichold for *The Penrose Annual*, 1938. Reduced. Original blocked in white on black.
Title-page designed by Tschichold for *The Penrose Annual*, 1938.

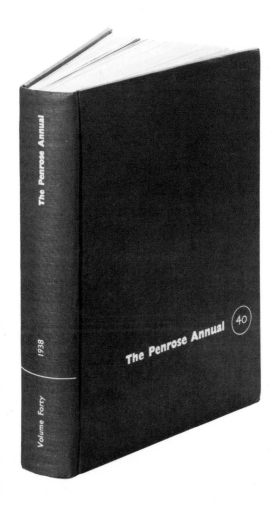

The Penrose Annual

Review of the Graphic Arts   *Edited by* R. B. Fishenden, *M.Sc.* (*Tech.*), F.R.P.S.

Volume Forty | 1938

LUND HUMPHRIES *&* CO. LTD.   12 Bedford Square, London, W.1

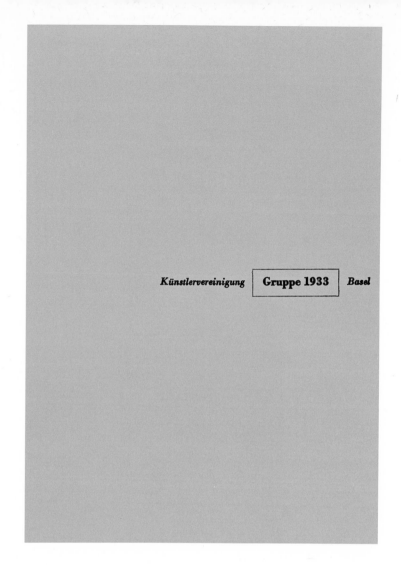

first time that typography, *per se*, had excited me. I was helped by finding German a not completely strange language; but, essentially, this was the first time that I appreciated the sensitive arrangement of small sizes of type, disposed according to a discernible and logical system and not by haphazard impulse. Among these specimens was the yellow paper-covered A4 size booklet *Typographische Entwurfstechnik* ('How to draw layouts'), 1932, which had an immediate appeal, since I had never yet received any systematic teaching in typography and could at last see, from the author's very clear drawings, how to draw a layout.

I was so impressed that I wrote to Tschichold, and, in July 1939, used my vacation to go to Basle to meet him. He took me to a café-restaurant beside the

Adolf Weißkopf: Skulptur 1936/37

Mit dem Ausdruck *gegenständliche Malerei* kann man Verschiedenes und zwar Sehr-Verschiedenes meinen, ja er scheint in jeweils anderer Bedeutung auf jede Malerei anzuwenden zu sein. Er kann in einem weiten Sinne denjenigen großen Teil aller Malerei bezeichnen, der überhaupt von etwas Vorgegebenem, etwas anderem Ersten ein Bild gibt, ein Bild gibt, indem er «darstellt» (abbildet, wiedergibt) oder aber auch indem er «ausdrückt» oder symbolisiert oder allegorisiert. Gegenstand ist in diesem Sinne der «dargestellte» handgreifliche Topf mit Blumen, aber auch die «ausgedrückte» geistige Beschaffenheit des Portraitierten, gegenständlich hier also etwa auch die, in einem anderen Sinne «ungegenständliche» Malerei Kandinskys, wenigstens die frühere, die durchaus etwas «ausdrücken» will. Schwer ist es, auszumachen, wie weit hier immer unter «Gegenstand» «Gegenstand an sich selber» und «Zum Gegenstand der Darstellung, der Expression usw. Gemachtes» verstanden wird. Man kann «gegenständliche Malerei» in diesem Sinne auch «naturalistisch» nennen, denn der Maler pflegt das Vorgegebene ganz allgemein «Natur» zu nennen, auch dann, wenn man sonst nicht von «Natur» reden würde: er malt nicht nur die Blume, sondern auch den Blumentopf «nach der Natur». Das Gegenteil «gegenständlicher Malerei» in diesem ersten Sinne ist «abstrakte Malerei», eine Formel, die hier beibehalten wird, weil sie gebräuchlich, nicht weil sie gut ist. Sie ist schlecht, weil sie von der Idee einer «naturalistischen Malerei» her gebildet ist: «abstrakte Malerei» ist so «abstrakt», wie ein Telephonapparat «abstrakt» ist, und ferner ist zu bedenken, ob nicht auch ein Wandanstrich, eine Autolackierung, die Streifen

12

13

Double spread from *Gruppe 1933* catalogue.

Rhine, where we sat for a summer's evening, drinking wine and attempting to exchange ideas on typography. My German and his English could hardly stretch to a whole evening of this, and I began to notice the glances of girls at nearby tables who, I realized, were wondering why we did not invite them to dance; but I did not dare mention this. We continued to discuss typography, and, when words failed, to beam at one another. I took back with me some more examples of Tschichold's work and we continued to correspond. Within a few days war broke out, and I did not return to printing for over six years. My first visit to Europe after the war was to spend my war gratuity skiing in Switzerland, and coming home, I found by coincidence Tschichold on the same train, on his way to join Penguin Books.

Poster designed by Tschichold, 1937. Reduced.
Original in black and sand-grey on white paper.

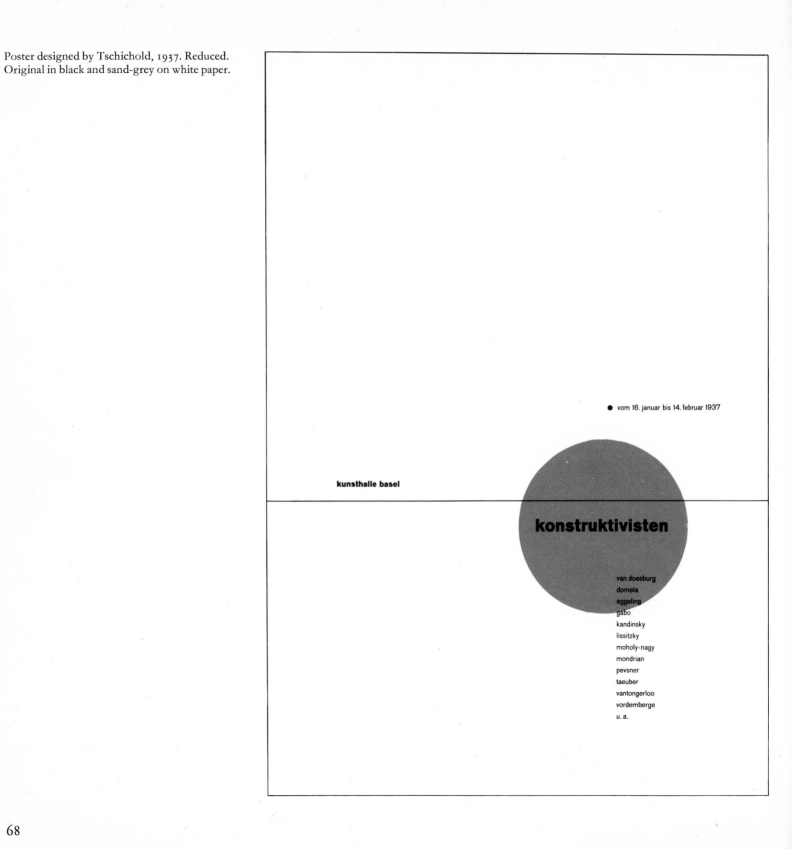

When Tschichold first went to Switzerland in 1933, and for many years afterwards, his work was almost entirely confined to designing books. He had few opportunities to design posters or commercial 'jobbing' and advertising. Asymmetric typography is in fact far less suitable for books than for jobbing. Tschichold began to find more and more that asymmetrical treatment was wrong for the books he was given to design. In addition he found, since the Swiss are very conventional, that his publisher clients were not sympathetic to advanced asymmetric typography. He was, all this time, under constant fear of losing his work permit and even permission to stay in Switzerland. But thinking over his clash with the Nazis opened his eyes to something else. 'To my astonishment', he wrote later,[1] 'I detected most shocking parallels between the teachings of *Die neue Typographie* and National Socialism and Fascism. Obvious similarities consist in the ruthless restriction of type-faces, a parallel to Goebbel's infamous "Gleichschaltung" ('Political alignment') and the more or less military arrangement of lines.' Tschichold's refusal to work for the Nazis in any capacity whatever, or to subscribe to their doctrines, whether political or typographical, had cost him his living in his own country. In Switzerland, he was free to develop his ideas in any direction he wished, but he had also to support a wife and child. His artistic and personal integrity were absolute; but the hard facts of economic and political life may have led him more quickly to a realization that in typographic design, asymmetry and symmetry can and must live together. They are not mutually exclusive philosophies but different ways of achieving one end.

In mid 1934, he published an article on margins (see p. 123) 'Die Anordnung des Schriftsatzes im Flächenraum' – 'The placing of type in a given space' in the Swiss printing journal *Typographische Monatsblätter*, No.7, in which he discussed and showed examples of the use of space round printed matter. Rules governing the placing of asymmetrical composition were formulated, but symmetrical composition was also illustrated. Morris's dictum that a book consists of not one but a pair of pages was ignored, since all the illustrations were of single pages. Among the conclusions he recommended were that, if designing asymmetrically, it is better to place a column of type closer to the right of the page rather than to the left, and that the amount of margin at the right should always be greater than the amount of space between words in the line.

In April 1935, Tschichold made his first public admission that centred typography was acceptable: in an article 'The design of centred typography' ('Vom richtigen Satz auf Mittelachse') in *Typographische Monatsblätter*, No.4. (see p. 126). All the illustrations are of centred layouts; many of the typographical rules he laid down – e.g., that matter should be arranged in groups, and that the eye can assimilate two or even three groups, but that with more than three, a page will lose clarity – apply equally to symmetric and asymmetric composition. Certainly

1 From Tschichold's statement at the 'Typography USA' seminar in New York, 1959. Reprinted in *Print XVIII*, no. 1, New York, 1964. (see p. 155).

SCHWEIZERISCHE ZOLLVERWALTUNG · ADMINISTRATION DES DOUANES SUISSES · AMMINISTRAZIONE DELLE DOGANE SVIZZERE

Postausfuhr
Exportation, poste
Esportazione, posta

No. 20

Deklaration[1]
Déclaration[1]
Dichiarazione[1]

No. _____

32933

Nachdruck verboten – Reproduction interdite – Riproduzione proibita

Land des Verbrauchs Pays de consommation Paese di consumo	Gattung der Ware – Nature de la marchandise Natura della merce	Gebrauchstarif Tarif d'usage Tariffa d'uso		Nettogewicht Poids net Peso netto	Stückzahl[1] Nombre de pièces[2] Numero dei capi[2]	Wert[3] Schweizer Fr. Valeur[3] Frs. suisses Valore[3] Fr. svizzeri
		No.	Litera	Kg.		Fr.

Anleitung auf der Rückseite – Instruction au dos – Istruzione a tergo

Anzahl der Begleitadressen
Nombre des bulletins d'expédition }——————— 4
Numero dei bollettini di spedizione

Ort und Datum
Lieu et date }
Località e data

┌───┐
│ **Raum zum Aufkleben der Wertzeichen**   │
│ **für die statistische Gebühr**   │
│ Espace destiné aux timbres-poste pour le droit de statistique │
│ Spazio per incollarvi i francobolli per la tassa di statistica │
└───┘

Unterschrift des Exporteurs
Signature de l'exportateur }
Firma dell'esportatore

Straße
Rue }
Strada

No. _____

1 Deklaration zu Handen der schweizerischen Zollverwaltung für die handelsstatistischen Erhebungen.
2 Nur für Schuhe (Paarzahl); Schreibmaschinen; Meterzahl für Filme.
3 Wirklicher Handelswert, nicht Versicherungswert.
4 Vom Exporteur auszufüllen.

1 Déclaration pour les relevés de la statistique du commerce, reste en mains de l'Administration des douanes suisses.
2 Pour chaussures (paires); machines à écrire; nombre de mètres pour films.
3 Valeur commerciale réelle, non pas valeur d'assurance.
4 A remplir par l'exportateur.

1 Dichiarazione per la statistica commerciale, rimane in possesso dell'amministrazione delle dogane svizzere.
2 Soltanto per scarpe (paia); macchine da scrivere; numero dei metri per film.
3 Valore reale commerciale e non valore di assicurazione.
4 Da riempirsi dall'esportatore.

Form designed by Tschichold for the Swiss Customs, 1938. Actual size. Original in black on pink.

[2] In addition to his drawn lettering for spines of books for Insel-Verlag and other publishers, which, as stated above, had always been centred.

from 1935, and possibly even earlier, Tschichold was designing some of his work symmetrically;[2] but to publish an article advocating symmetrical typography must have appeared to be a complete *volte-face*. It was not in fact so; but the vehemence and persuasiveness with which he had previously advocated asymmetrical typography had won him many disciples, who simply could not now change their own minds. Tschichold was not now saying that his theories of asymmetrical typography were wrong: he admitted he was wrong only in so far as he had said, or implied, that symmetrical typography was dead, finished, decadent, and immoral in the middle of the twentieth century. But certain of his converts never forgave him and have not done so to this day.

Nevertheless, the plain fact is that typographic design is subject to certain basic principles – and Tschichold was the first to spell them out clearly – which apply equally to centred or asymmetric systems. Both systems have their advantages and disadvantages and a good designer will decide which offers the better solution to the problem at hand. No teacher has ever explained more clearly than Tschichold the merits and demerits of each system. Tschichold's move away from his previously uncompromising position as a prophet of the modern movement caused much controversy and he was bitterly attacked, particularly by the Swiss sculptor Max Bill. Finally, Tschichold wrote an article 'Glaube und Wirklichkeit' ('Belief and Reality') which besides answering Bill, was a highly important statement about typography in general. It was published in *Schweizer Graphische Mitteilungen* in June 1946, and a translation of it appears for the first time in English among the appendices of this book (see p. 131).

Another most interesting comment on Tschichold's change of direction occurs in a letter by Kurt Schwitters written from England in 1946 to Nelly Van Doesburg. It in fact says more about Schwitters than Tschichold. Schwitters wrote: 'I am sorry about Tschichold's reactionar work. But look, it is impossible to do revolutionar work for a long time without coming in a state as Delaunay. I myself devellop portraitpainting for remaining fit for abstract painting and sculpture. If you stand alone for a long time on a way, where only few people follow you, you must do something of that thing. For not getting mad. Tschichold has worked so long time and so many times modern typography, that he is week and would do it now without feeling. Therefore he does good to work for a time in old style. I always did portraits therefore I am not weak in doing revolutionar work on and on.' (Schwitters to Nelly Van Doesburg, written from Ambleside,[3] 10 September 1946).

It may be possible for the designer of a book about modern art to make the design of the work itself a statement on modern art – as in fact Tschichold did with such works as *foto-auge* and *Fototek I* – but not all books are on modern art. Tschichold was now practising as a general book designer, whose designs must respect and serve the texts he is given.

All typographic design depends on nuances: the difference between a pleasing and an ugly page may be measured in points or millimetres. The designer has to juggle with type sizes and weights which differ from each other by minute amounts, but these amounts are critical; so are the amounts of white space in which he places his black or coloured lines, and which he uses to relate the groups, masses, letters, dots or drawings which he has to position. It can be said that symmetrical typography is traditional, and asymmetric is 'modern'; but it is

[3] from *Holland Dada*, by K. Schippers. Querido, Amsterdam, 1974. I am grateful to Herbert Spencer for calling my attention to this.

Letter-heading designed by Tschichold for
Philobiblon, Vienna.

philobiblon eine zeitschrift für bücherliebhaber . a magazine for book-collectors

herbert reichner verlag, wien VI (vienna), strohmayergasse 6

telephon	b 23854
bankkonto	wiener bankverein, wien XIV
postscheckkonten	leipzig 8442
	wien 46469
	prag 501701
	zürich VII 18122

perfectly possible, using a centred layout, to make an uncompromisingly modern design. It is sometimes difficult to make an asymmetric design using a shield or symbol (which itself is normally symmetric) – especially in a narrow space such as the spine of a book. If one is designing a style which must suit a whole set of books, one often finds that a centred style is more practical – Tschichold decided that when asked to set a style for the Birkhäuser Classics in Basle in 1941, and again for Penguin Books in 1946. It may have had something to do with the feeling of the times, and what was wanted (or would be accepted) by the public for whom he was working. Later, in the 1960s, another designer decided that Penguin typography should be asymmetric, and as far as I know that decision was accepted as happily by the Penguin public as had been Tschichold's. The problem of whether to choose a symmetric or asymmetric style always has to be faced when one is designing a house style for a firm. The designer usually has to design a system which can be applied by unskilled people obeying a set of rules; there may easily be hundreds, even thousands, of different letter headings and forms, constantly requiring changes, as when directors and addresses are changed, and the skilled designer cannot for the rest of his life be available to make every small adjustment. In such a case, an asymmetric system will almost certainly be more flexible and easier to organize under rules than a centred system.

Examples of the work Tschichold did for Benno Schwabe, Holbein and Birkhäuser, and other Swiss publishers between 1933 and the end of the war are shown on pp.59–84. The Birkhäuser Classics, for which he designed some 53 volumes, were his biggest and most successful commission. These were a series of almost pocket volumes which included a ten-volume Shakespeare and a twelve-volume Goethe. They were admired by Oliver Simon in London, among others, and provided the best proof of his capabilities when Allen Lane later asked Simon whom he should ask to undertake the redesign of Penguin Books after the war. The Birkhäuser Classics were issued both with linen spines and patterned paper sides, and in full linen, and sometimes in leather; they were highly elegant although produced for a mass market, and sold at the then extremely low price of 3 francs a volume. Every title was individually designed by Tschichold. He also designed the 'Sammlung Birkhäuser' (Birkhäuser Collection), another series in smaller format, of which he edited some titles. These were also beautifully designed (see p.74), in decorative paper covers, although they were not conceived as paper-backs in today's sense.

During his first years in Switzerland, Tschichold had to spend much of his time writing books and articles: writing on typography was an activity on which there were no official restrictions. In 1940 he published *Der frühe chinesische Farbendruck* Holbein-Verlag Basle (*Early Chinese Colour Printing* The Beechhurst Press, New York, Allen & Unwin, London, 1953), the first of a series of works written and

73

DES LUIGI DA PORTO
GESCHICHTE
VON ROMEO UND JULIA

SAMMLUNG BIRKHÄUSER

edited by him on this subject, after his wife had found for him a fine copy of an early edition, dated 1715, of the famous Ten Bamboo Studio. His last published work was also on Chinese Colour Printing: *Die Bildersammlung der Zehnbambushalle* (Eugen Rentsch Verlag, Erlenbach, Switzerland, 1970), published in English as *Chinese Colour Prints from the Ten Bamboo Studio* (Lund Humphries, London, and McGraw Hill, New York, 1972).

His authority as a writer on typography and book design was further enhanced by *Geschichte der Schrift in Bildern*, Holbein-Verlag, Basle 1941, which was published in English by Zwemmer in 1946 as *An Illustrated History of Writing and Lettering*; by *Gute Schriftformen* (*Good Letter Forms*), Basle 1941/2, *Schriftkunde, Schreibübungen und Skizzieren für Setzer* (*Type faces, Lettering and Layout*

CONSTANTIN
SILENS

—

IRRWEG
UND
UMKEHR

—

Betrachtungen

über

das Schicksal

Deutschlands

—

Birkhäuser

CONSTANTIN SILENS

IRRWEG
UND UMKEHR

Betrachtungen
über das Schicksal
Deutschlands

BIRKHÄUSER

det worden, das heißt so, daß das abgekürzte Bild eines Begriffs, der mit einem beſtimmten Laut begann, nur für diesen Anfangslaut, ſtatt für den Begriff, gesetzt wurde. So entſtand zum Beispiel das O aus einem mit o beginnenden Wort für Auge. Es hat nichts mit dem geöffneten Munde zu tun, wie man manchmal meint. Das M entwickelte sich aus einem wellenförmigen Zeichen für Wasser. Der Gebrauch dieser Lautzeichen hat den Weg der abendländischen Bildung entschieden.

Die alten Griechen gebrauchten schon die meiſten unserer Großbuchſtaben; doch hatten nicht alle den gleichen Lautwert wie die Zeichen unseres Alphabets. P zum Beispiel bezeichnete den Laut r. Diese Formen wurden von den Römern übernommen, einigen aber, den Bedürfnissen der la-

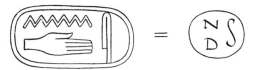

Die älteste Lautzeichenschrift, die auf uns gekommen iſt, und ihr phonetischer Wert. Hieroglyphische Lautzeichen. Um 4000 v. Chr. Das Zeichen für « Send», einen König der 2. Dynaſtie. Ashmolean Museum, Oxford. Nach Johnſton.

teinischen Sprache gemäß, ein anderer Lautwert zuerteilt. Noch andere Buchſtaben, wie G und R, wurden neu gebildet.

Die älteren griechischen Inschriften zeigen sehr einfache geometrische Formen – Kreise, Dreiecke und rechteckige Figuren –, Strichformen, die anfänglich mit ritzenden Inſtrumenten erzeugt worden waren. Schon die gemeißelten Buchſtaben *römischer Inschriften* der klassischen Zeit verraten aber im Umriß ihrer Einzelteile die Vorzeichnung mit einem flachpinselartigen Werkzeug, das im Wechsel dicke und dünne Striche (Bandzüge) ergibt. Aus dem addierenden Ritzen der Frühzeit hatten sich rhythmische Bewegungen entwickelt. Der europäische Mensch begann zu schreiben.

Dennoch waren die altrömischen Buchſtaben noch keine wirkliche Schreibschrift. Ihre geometrischen Formen müssen zusammengesetzt werden und sind nicht eigentlich schreibgerecht. Geschriebener Rhythmus wurde nur dort erreicht, wo schneller und kleiner geschrieben wurde als

Griechische Inschrift. Athen, 6. Jahrhundert v. Chr.

Klassische Form der römischen Kapitalschrift. Um 114 n. Chr.

Schrift

EIN LEHRBUCH DER SCHRIFT

kunde

VON JAN TSCHICHOLD

Schreib

FÜR SETZER

übungen

GRAPHIKER UND FREUNDE

und

GUTER SCHRIFT

Skizzieren

E·R·WEISS SCHRIEB DEM VERFASSER ÜBER DIESES BUCH: SEIEN SIE HERZLICH BEDANKT FÜR DAS NEUE SCHRIFTBUCH · MAN KANN DAS NICHT BESSER MACHEN, IN JEDER BEZIEHUNG ✳ STANLEY MORISON SCHRIEB: LIKE ALL YOUR PUBLICATIONS, YOUR NEW BOOK ON TYPOGRAPHY AND LAYOUT IS MOST PLEASINGLY WRITTEN AND PRINTED · THE BOOK GAINS A GREAT DEAL TOO FROM YOUR OWN CALLIGRAPHY ✳

Title-page designed by Tschichold for a title in the 'Sammlung Birkhäuser' series, 1945.

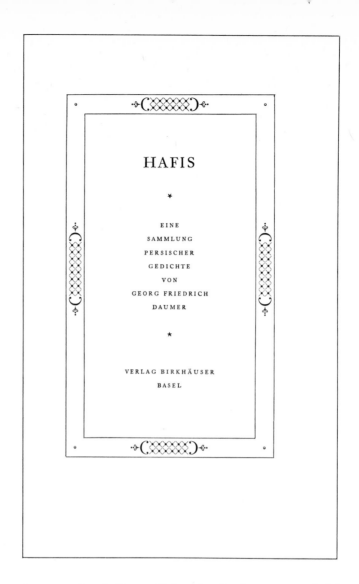

HAFIS

✴

EINE
SAMMLUNG
PERSISCHER
GEDICHTE
VON
GEORG FRIEDRICH
DAUMER

★

VERLAG BIRKHÄUSER
BASEL

for compositors), Benno Schwabe, Basle, 1942, and *Schatzkammer der Schreibkunst* (*A Treasury of Calligraphy*), Birkhäuser, Basle, 1945. *Gute Schriftformen* (*Good Letter Forms*) was published by the Education Department of the City of Basle, and consists of six A4-size booklets, collected in a canvas-sided portfolio, each containing sixteen pages of photographs of manuscripts, inscriptions and book pages, and specimens of type-faces, together with, in the first booklet, some of the basic rules of typography – altogether an admirable introduction for young compositors and printing apprentices. These booklets, incidentally, were designed in the traditional centred style, as was everything by Tschichold by this time.

Schriftkunde, etc. is an eighty-page book in octavo format, printed on art paper and bound in gold-blocked brown Ingres paper on boards; it was reprinted in an expanded form in 1951 in Germany but has never been translated into English. It

HOMERS
WERKE
I
ODYSSEE

—

ÜBERSETZT
VON
JOHANN
HÉINRICH
VOSS

BIRKHÄUSER-
KLASSIKER

24

HOMERS ODYSSEE

ÜBERSETZT VON JOH. HEINR. VOSS (1781)
HERAUSGEGEBEN UND EINGELEITET
VON PETER VON DER MÜHLL

Wohl kaum eine andere Dichtung verdient eher durch eine wohlfeile aber würdige Ausgabe weitesten Kreisen zugänglich gemacht zu werden, als das unvergängliche Frühwerk der europäischen Literatur, des Griechen Homer Epos von den Irrfahrten des Odysseus und seiner Heimkehr nach Ithaka. Zu viele noch kennen nicht mehr als den blossen Umriss der alten Fabel, wie ihn der Geschichtsunterricht vermittelt. Ihre ganze Schönheit enthüllt diese wahrhaft wundervolle Dichtung des Altertums indessen nur dem, der sie in gebundener Fassung liest. Johann Heinrich Voss, der Zeitgenosse Goethes, hat ihr die langersehnte deutsche Form verliehen. Seine Hexameter erstrahlen auch heute noch in jugendlicher Frische und sind die gültige Übersetzung des Gebildeten geblieben. Kein schöneres Geschenk für einen jungen Menschen, kein Werk, das auch dem reifen Manne eine grössere geistige Erquickung gewährt.

VERLAG BIRKHÄUSER BASEL   3 Fr.

ARNOLD VON SALIS

ANTIKE UND RENAISSANCE

ÜBER NACHLEBEN UND WEITERWIRKEN
DER ALTEN IN DER NEUEREN KUNST

MIT 136 ABBILDUNGEN AUF 64 TAFELN

EUGEN RENTSCH VERLAG · ERLENBACH-ZÜRICH

GOTTFRIED GUGGENBÜHL

GESCHICHTE
DER
SCHWEIZERISCHEN
EIDGENOSSEN-
SCHAFT

ERSTER BAND
VON DEN ANFÄNGEN BIS
ZUM JAHRE 1648

EUGEN RENTSCH VERLAG

Prospectus for *Schatzkammer der Schreibkunst,*
1945. Reduced. Original in black and red.

SCHATZKAMMER DER SCHREIBKUNST

MEISTERWERKE DER KALLIGRAPHIE AUS VIER JAHRHUNDERTEN AUF ZWEIHUNDERT TAFELN

AUSGEWÄHLT UND EINGELEITET VON JAN TSCHICHOLD

VERLAG BIRKHÄUSER · BASEL · MCMXLV

SCHATZKAMMER DER SCHREIBKUNST

MEISTERWERKE DER KALLIGRAPHIE AUS VIER JAHRHUNDERTEN

AUSGEWÄHLT UND EINGELEITET VON JAN TSCHICHOLD

VERLAG BIRKHÄUSER · BASEL

Book-jacket designed by Tschichold, 1944. Actual size. Original in black and red on ochre.

HUGO BALL

DIE FLUCHT AUS DER ZEIT

is, again, an admirable and handy little introduction to the knowledge of lettering and type, beautifully designed and printed: no such book existed in England at that time. Stanley Morison's *Type Designs of the Past and Present*, 1926, covered a little of the same ground but was purely historical in intention; Eric Gill's *An Essay on Typography* (limited edition 1931; second edition, unlimited, 1936), although certainly concerned with problems of design was, like Tschichold's earlier books, intended to be provocative and serves a different purpose. Like Tschichold's books, it is also exciting to look at and handle. Oliver Simon's *An Introduction to Typography*, again not a close parallel, was not published until 1945.

Schatzkammer der Schreibkunst was a magnificent landscape volume of 200 plates (page size 242 × 330 mm) showing masterpieces of calligraphy from Vicentino (Arrighi), 1522, to Heinrigs of Cologne, 1831, and four pages of Midolle from 1834 to 1840 (Hermann Degering's comparable anthology of lettering did not venture into the nineteenth century).

Between 1939 and 1945 Tschichold also wrote at least eight articles in Swiss graphic art periodicals. In 1942, he was awarded citizenship of the City of Basle, rarely granted during the war years. He was no longer a refugee and could earn his living as he liked.

Trimmed page area 7 1/16" x 4 3/4".
Size of boards 4 3/4" x 7 1/4, fibre direction to be parallel to spine.
(without cover)
Hinge 1/8".

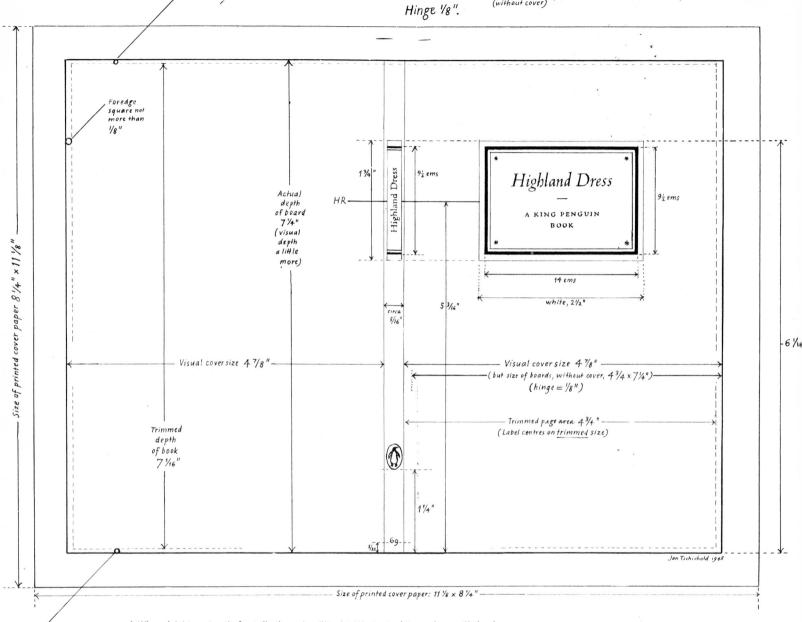

Top square 3/32"

Foredge square not more than 1/8"

Actual depth of board 7 1/4" (visual depth a little more)

Size of printed cover paper 8 1/4" x 11 1/8"

Trimmed depth of book 7 1/16"

Visual cover size 4 7/8"

1 3/4"

HR

Highland Dress

9 1/2 ems

circa 5/16"

5 3/16"

Highland Dress
A KING PENGUIN BOOK

9 1/2 ems

14 ems

white, 2 1/2"

Visual cover size 4 7/8"
(but size of boards, without cover, 4 3/4 x 7 1/4")
(hinge = 1/8")

Trimmed page area 4 3/4"
(Label centres on trimmed size)

1 1/4"

69

5/32

6 1/8"

Jan Tschichold 1948

Tail square 3/32"

Size of printed cover paper: 11 1/8" x 8 1/4"

1. When a label is used on the front, its size and position should be in complete accordance with the above.
2. The lettering on the labels not to be drawn but in type, in harmony with the type used in the book.
3. Position and style of the spine label, when used, is the same throughout the series, with the thickness altered if necessary, according to the thickness of the book.
4. If there is no label proper on the front, try to avoid a label on the spine and centre lettering to the horizontal rule HR.
5. The position of the King Penguin sign is unalterable. It must appear within a black-bordered oval if there is a label on the spine or its background does not allow for an unbordered sign, but otherwise it should appear without an oval. Good photographs of the design wanted are obtainable from the Penguin Office.
6. The number to appear on the bottom as indicated. Its position is unalterable. Size: 9 pt. No "K".

Chapter 5 Penguin Books 1947-49

The 'grid' or standard instructions for King Penguin covers (paper on boards), devised and drawn by Tschichold, 1948. Reduced.

The Second World War ended with the defeat of Germany and Japan in 1945. All over the world men and women could go back to the lives and careers that had been interrupted in 1939. In England and America book publishers had been required to restrict both the bulk and quality of paper and the size of margins in order to save paper. They were now able to think of returning to pre-war standards of design and production. Penguin Books had special problems. The first batch of Penguins had been published on 30 July, 1935, familiar titles in a then unfamiliar red-white-red paper-back form, sold at sixpence each. The estimated break-even figure was 17,500 copies per title. Within three years the firm 'had ceased considering any figure less than 50,000, and that only as a first printing order' (*Penguins: A Retrospect: 1935–1951*). During the war, when admittedly it was easy to sell anything printed on paper, Penguin Books went everywhere with English-speaking or reading service men and women and were a solace that only the people who lived through that period can fully understand. By the beginning of 1945 nearly 500 titles in Penguins, 150 in Pelicans, and numerous other series had appeared, and the minds of Allen Lane and his colleagues were full of ideas for new projects. Allen Lane consulted many people on whom he should hire to handle his design, and was characteristically determined to have no one but the best. It was Oliver Simon who suggested inviting Jan Tschichold over from Switzerland. I believe that everyone else whom Allen Lane asked said that it was not necessary to invite a foreigner, there was plenty of typographic talent in Britain. It was a measure of Lane's genius that, as on many other occasions, he rejected the advice of the majority, followed his intuition, and was proved right. Not that Tschichold was at that time an unknown quantity, for he was certainly the leading practising book designer in Europe and, many thought, in the world. Allen Lane and Oliver Simon flew to Basle in September 1946[1] and invited Tschichold to come to England and become the Penguin typographer. He accepted but was not able to give up his Swiss commitments and come to London until March 1947.

[1] 'I had the pleasure to see here fourteen days ago Allen Lane and Oliver Simon.' Letter from J. T. to A. Fairbank dated 15 September, 1946.

Right: the Penguin cover as Tschichold found it in 1947. Reduced. This was Penguin no.331, first published in 1941.
Opposite: Tschichold's first revision of the Penguin cover, with the Penguin symbol redrawn, following quite closely the original bird drawn by Edward Young in 1935, and Tschichold's next refinement in the standard Penguin cover, 1949.

Before he came over, Tschichold had asked for a copy of every single piece of printed paper used by Penguins, as well as for examples of all their books. He annotated every single one, as well as all the books, with his criticisms in pencil, and these comments, circulated to editorial staff before he arrived, were a typographic education in themselves.

Tschichold's task was formidable. The problem of designing for mass production was something he had been thinking and writing about all his working life, and now, at the age of 45, he had the biggest opportunity that existed in publishing to do it. Previous typographers had done it before – e.g. Morison for Gollancz, Mardersteig for Albatross – but never on such a scale, with so many different series involved. It was the first time that any typographer had ever had such a task in the modern machine age. The chief qualities of too

many English typographers at that time were romantic and amateur. Stanley Morison, who was neither, and who understood perfectly the implications of mass production, was too heavily engaged in other important industrial and editorial activities to have considered taking on Penguins, and very probably no one else but Tschichold would have been capable of it. It required a tireless attention to detail, an unshakable belief in the rightness of his principles, an ability to systematize and to remain consistently faithful to the systems, and a thick skin. The arguments and complaints against Tschichold's innovations and so-called Germanic regimentation, which affected and disturbed (but generally failed to wake up) nearly every major printing firm in Britain, since most of them worked at least occasionally for Penguins, were at first many; but Tschichold knew just enough English to announce his views and could look innocently uncomprehending if anyone tried to argue against them.

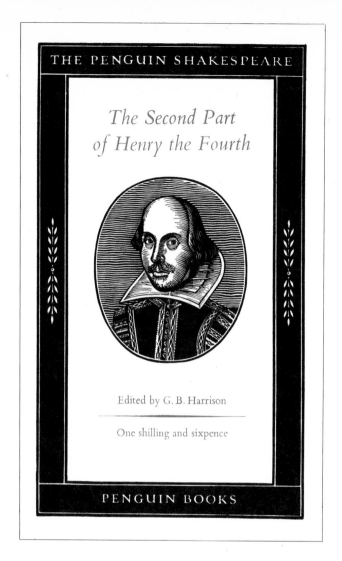

Tschichold, appointed typographer to Penguin Books, took immediate and complete control of every single item of printed matter in the business. One of the first things he tackled was composition, for which he formulated the Penguin Composition Rules, reproduced on pp.94–5. Their importance to the British printing trade as a whole cannot be overemphasized. Today, a quarter of a century later, they are still exactly valid, and still have to be insisted on: ignorance and carelessness of typographic detail are still regrettably common in British printing. Tschichold's rules deserve to be read closely: word by word and to the end. It will be seen that their aim is not to promote a designer's aesthetic whims but to aid pleasing communication between author and reader – which is, after all, what typographic design is all about. Next he provided grids for all the series: an example is shown on p.86. A 'grid' had not previously been made for Penguin Books. A 'grid' is merely the laying-down of exact instructions for,

Cover designed by Tschichold for the Penguin Poets series, 1949. Reduced. Original in black and green on light green paper.

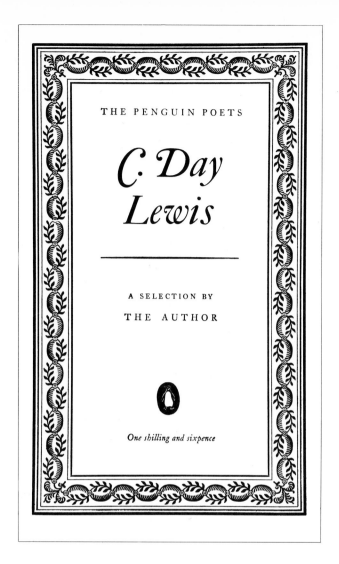

THE PENGUIN POETS

C. Day Lewis

A SELECTION BY

THE AUTHOR

One shilling and sixpence

first, the trimmed page size of a book, and secondly, the positioning of margins, and such things as titles, symbols, series numbers and prices. The King Penguin series provide a good example of the sort of production design problem that Tschichold had to tackle. They were small books, the same depth but slightly wider than ordinary Penguins, but bound in paper on boards, and (from a certain date) jacketed. They were originally conceived as always containing colour plates, on the pattern of the Insel-Verlag picture books; but, like the Insel books, they sometimes had only monochrome plates. The 'normal' pattern was thirty-two pages of text and thirty-two pages of plates, but this was often varied. They sold (after the war) at *2s 6d*. It is doubtful if they ever made a profit; they were one of many series planned idealistically by Allen Lane and continued because they were pleasing and prestigious, but they were subsidized from the profits of the ordinary Penguins.

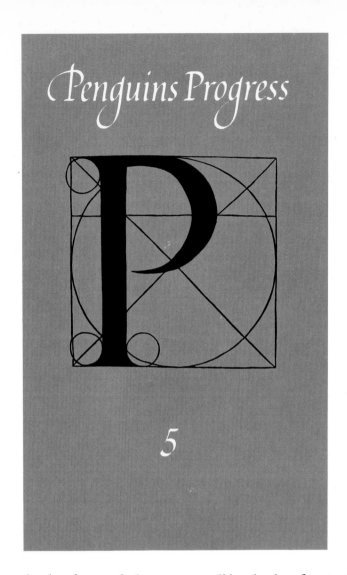

As already stated, they were small books, but five or six different factories might be involved in the manufacture of one title. The text might be printed by one firm in letterpress, the monochrome plates by another firm in photo-litho; the colour plates and coloured covers by one or two others, and the binding handled by yet another. The paper would certainly be supplied by another, possibly by two or even three other firms. The designer and production manager had therefore to work very closely together, and, before Tschichold arrived, no one had effectively tackled the problem of unifying and co-ordinating the efforts of the participating manufacturers from the point of view of design. Tschichold was also well equipped to advise on the technical aspects of production and frequently did so.

Having established basic rules for composition, which affected, and gradually improved, the style of text setting for every line of type in every Penguin book – eventually achieving a standard which can only be called impeccable, and which, because it spread to printing firms all over Great Britain who printed for Penguins, improved the standard of book composition throughout the British publishing trade, Tschichold turned his attention to the actual design of the books. He started with the popular standard Penguin cover, and by means of a few small alterations considerably improved it. At the same time, he found that the Penguin symbol itself existed in several variations, more or less unauthorized and used indiscriminately, so he redrew it, and also the Pelican, Puffin and other symbols then in use. His attention was then turned to the covers of Pelicans, the designation of non-fiction titles which had the same basic cover design as Penguins, printed in pale blue. Originally all reprints, this series now consisted mostly of new and specially-commissioned books, many of them illustrated, for which the completely standardized three-horizontal-panel cover was no longer flexible enough. Tschichold devised a variety of styles to accommodate varying requirements, but keeping the blue colour as the sign of the series (illustration on p. 101). He completely redesigned the Penguin Shakespeare series, making it perhaps the most distinguished of all his Penguin designs, although it has strong competition from the Penguin Poets covers (illustration on p. 91). Then there were Penguin Prints, Penguin Specials, Penguin Reference Books, Penguin Music Scores, and many others. The stream (not large, but continuous) of King Penguins gave Tschichold more scope than most of the other series, since every title was different in design and gave opportunity for more decorative treatment (see illustrations on pp. 96–7). Then there were the Puffin series for children. The present writer, who had joined Penguin Books in 1946, was responsible for Puffin Picture books, a children's series of landscape books, usually of thirty-two pages, including self covers, $7\frac{1}{4} \times 8\frac{5}{8}$ in., and edited by Noel Carrington, who commissioned the art-work: every page was illustrated, and usually the alternate openings (i.e., one side of the sheet) were printed in full colour. Many of the artists drew their illustrations direct onto litho plates or onto transparent film; others drew for photographic reproduction by either letterpress, photo-litho, or photogravure. The type matter had to be fitted into the spaces left for it in the artists' art-work. I worked in an office next door to Tschichold's and I often took the art-work received from the artists into Tschichold's office in despair, showing him that it had been drawn in the wrong size or wrong proportions, and wanting to send it back. Time and again, Tschichold pointed out a way of adapting the art-work so that the finished job often looked even better than if it had been drawn correctly. To have sent the art-work back to the artist, requesting him to redraw it in the size he had been told, would have resulted in arguments, delays, extra costs, and certainly, in some cases, no book.

Penguin Composition Rules

TEXT COMPOSITION

All text composition should be as closely word-spaced as possible. As a rule, the spacing should be about a middle space or the thickness of an 'i' in the type size used.

Wide spaces should be strictly avoided. Words may be freely broken whenever necessary to avoid wide spacing, as breaking words is less harmful to the appearance of the page than too much space between words.

All major punctuation marks – full point, colon, and semicolon – should be followed by the same spacing as is used throughout the rest of the line.

INDENTING OF PARAGRAPHS

The indent of the paragraph should be the em of the fount body.

Omit indents in the first line of the first paragraph of any text and at the beginning of a new section that comes under a subheading. It is not necessary to set the first word in small capitals, but if this is done for any reason, the word should be letter-spaced in the same way as the running title.

If a chapter is divided into several parts without headings, these parts should be divided not only by an additional space, but always by one or more asterisks of the fount body. As a rule, one asterisk is sufficient. Without them it is impossible to see whether a part ends at the bottom of a page or not. Even when the last line of such a part ends the page, there will always be space for an asterisk in the bottom margin.

PUNCTUATION MARKS AND SPELLING

If this can be done on the keyboard, put thin spaces before question marks, exclamation marks, colons, and semicolons.

Between initials and names, as in G. B. Shaw and after all abbreviations where a full point is used, use a smaller (fixed) space than between the other words in the line.

Instead of em rules without spaces, use en rules preceded and followed by the word space of the line, as in the third paragraph above.

Marks of omission should consist of three full points. These should be set without any spaces, but be preceded and followed by word spaces.

1

Use full points sparingly, and omit after these abbreviations: Mr, Mrs, Messrs, Dr, St, WC2, 8vo, and others containing the last letter of the abbreviated word.

Use single quotes for a first quotation and double quotes for quotations within quotations. If there is still another quotation within the second, return to single quotes. Punctuation belonging to a quotation comes within the quotes, otherwise outside.

Opening quotes should be followed by a hairspace except before A and J. Closing quotes should be preceded by a hairspace except after a comma or a full point. If this cannot be done on the keyboard, omit these hairspaces, but try to get the necessary attachment.

When long extracts are set in small type do not use quotes.

Use parentheses ( ) for explanation and interpolations; brackets [ ] for notes.

For all other queries on spelling, consult the *Rules for Compositors and Readers at the University Press, Oxford,* or Collins's *Authors' and Printers' Dictionary.*

CAPITALS, SMALL CAPITALS, AND ITALICS

Words in capitals must always be letter-spaced. The spacing of the capitals in lines of importance should be very carefully optically equalized. The word spaces in lines either of capitals or small capitals should not exceed an en quad.

All display lines set in the same fount should be given the same spacing throughout the book.

Use small capitals for running headlines and in contents pages. They must always be slightly letter-spaced to make words legible.

Running headlines, unless otherwise stated, should consist of the title of the book on the left-hand page, and the contents of the chapter on the right.

Italics are to be used for emphasis, for foreign words and phrases, and for the titles of books, newspapers, and plays which appear in the text. In such cases the definite article 'The' should be printed in roman, unless it is part of the title itself.

In bibliographical and related matter, as a rule, authors' names should be given in small capitals with capitals, and the titles in italics.

FIGURES

Do not mix old style text composition with modern face figures. Either hanging or ranging figures may be used if they are cut in the fount used for the text.

In text matter, numbers under 100 should be composed in letters. Use figures when the matter consists of a sequence of stated

2

94

quantities, particulars of age, &c. In dates use the fewest possible figures, 1946-7, not 1946-1947. Divide by an en rule without spaces.

REFERENCES AND FOOTNOTES

The reference to a footnote may be given by an asterisk of the fount body, if there are only a few footnotes in the book, and not more than one per page. But if there are two or more footnotes per page, use superior fraction figures preceded by a thin space.

Do not use modern face fraction figures in any old style fount. Either hanging or ranging fraction figures may be used provided that they are in harmony with the face used for the text. For books composed in any old face letter, we recommend Monotype Superior Figures F627, to be cast on the size two points below the size of the face used.

Footnotes should be set two points smaller than the text. Indent the first line of these with the same number of points as the paragraphs in the text matter. Use equal leading between all lines of footnotes, use the same leading as in the text matter, and put 1-2 point lead underneath the last line in order to get register with the normal lines.

For the numbering of footnotes use normal figures followed by a full point and an en quad. These figures may run either throughout the chapter, or even through the whole book, according to the special instructions given by the typographer.

FOLIOS

These should, as a rule, be set in the same size and face as the text, and in arabic numerals.

Pagination should begin with the first leaf in the book, but the first folio actually appearing is that on the verso of the first page of the text.

When there is preliminary matter whose extent is unknown at the time of making up the text into pages, it is necessary to use lower-case roman numerals, numbered from the first page of the first sheet. The first actually appearing cannot be definitely stated, but may be on the acknowledgements page, or at latest on the second page of the preface. In this case, the first arabic folio to appear will be '2' on the verso of the first text page.

Folios for any text matter at the end of the book, such as index &c., should continue the arabic numbering of the text pages.

THE PRINTING OF PLAYS

The same rules should apply to the printing of plays as to the printing of prose. Names of characters should be set in capitals

and small capitals. The text following is indented. Stage directions should be in italics, enclosed in square brackets. The headline should include the number of the act and the scene.

THE PRINTING OF POETRY

For printing poetry use type of a smaller size than would be used for prose. All composition should be leaded and the words evenly spaced with middle spaces. The titles should be centred on the measure, not on the first line. The beginning of each poem may be treated as a chapter opening, with small capitals, &c.

Extra leading, especially between verses of irregular length, may often be misleading, as it is impossible to see whether the verse ends at the bottom of the page or not. The safest way of recognizing the poet's intention is to indent the first line of every new verse, after which leading is not really necessary. Therefore, the first line of the second and following verses should be indented, unless the poet has indicated a shape not allowing for indentations.

MAKE-UP

Books should, with certain exceptions, be made up in the following order:

I. Preliminary pages: 1, half title; 2, frontispiece; 3, title; 4, Imprint or date of publication; 5, dedication; 6, acknowledgements; 7, contents; 8, list of illustrations; 9, list of abbreviations; 10, preface; 11, introduction; 12, errata.

II. The text of the book.

III. Additional matter: 1. appendix; 2. author's notes; 3. glossary; 4. bibliography; 5. index.

The above should each begin on a right-hand page, imprint and frontispiece excepted. As a rule, chapter headings should be dropped a few lines.

The preliminary pages should be set in the same face and style as the book itself. Avoid bold faces.

The index should be set in two or more columns and in type two points smaller than the text. The first word of each letter of the alphabet should be set in small capitals with capitals.

Jan Tschichold

POPULAR
ART
IN THE UNITED
STATES

— * ❃ * —

BY ERWIN O. CHRISTENSEN

WITH ILLUSTRATIONS

FROM THE

INDEX OF AMERICAN DESIGN

NATIONAL GALLERY OF ART

WASHINGTON, D.C.

— * ❃ * —

PENGUIN BOOKS

LONDON

It is interesting to note that although Tschichold laid down standards for every detail of Penguin layout that he thought needed them, he never standardized either the type-face or the layout of title-pages – as Morison had done, successfully, when he chose Baskerville type and a standard layout for Gollancz novels in the 1930s. The Penguin list included books of so many different kinds and characters, many with special features, such as poems or quotations or illustrations on the title-pages, and wide differences in length and in the forms of chapter organization and so on, that Tschichold decided to treat every book as a separate design problem. He therefore gave himself the freedom to choose for it the most suitable type-face (nearly always from the magnificent Monotype range planned by Morison) from those available at the particular printer contracted to print the book; and the treatment on the title-page it seemed to need. It was a formidable task, but it was a decision in line with Allen Lane's insistence on the highest quality of

SOME BRITISH

BEETLES

GEOFFREY TAYLOR

WITH COLOUR PLATES
BY
VERE TEMPLE

PENGUIN BOOKS
LONDON

everything to do with Penguins, beginning with the books they chose to publish: it was more respectful to the books themselves, chosen because they were literature, to treat them as individuals – which they were – rather than as products of a sausage machine.

Two King Penguin title-pages designed by Tschichold are reproduced here.

Even Tschichold did not know the exact number of title-pages he designed for Penguins: it was more than 500, and for many of them, ancillary pages such as lists of contents and chapter titles also required special layouts. The series which he either redesigned or designed *de novo* for Penguins, or of which he designed some individual titles, consisted of:

Penguin Books
Pelican Books
Penguin Classics
King Penguins
Penguin Modern Painters
Penguin Music Scores
New Biology
Science News
New Writing
Penguin Parade
Penguin Poets
Penguin Prints
Porpoise Books
Puffin Story and Picture Books
Penguin Reference Books
Penguin Shakespeare
Some Penguin and Pelican Specials
Some miscellaneous titles not in series
Pelican History of Art (prospectus and plate grid only)

Tschichold was in design charge of what was at that time one of the larger book publishing programmes in the world – the usual first printing order for a Penguin was not less than 50,000 copies and often much more – but although once a book was in the printer's hands it became a unit of mass-production, at the designing stage it was all hand-work: the layout for every title-page and other design was drawn by hand, and for many books, several designs would be tried and abandoned before the final solution was decided on. It is remarkable that Tschichold achieved this vast output with only one assistant, a young Dane, Erik Ellegaard Frederiksen, whom he appointed in 1948, after he had been working alone for about a year. Frederiksen worked with him for the rest of his time at Penguins, until December 1949.

In reply to questions from the author about this period, Frederiksen (who at that time had just finished his training, in Denmark) wrote:

'This period was the typographic foundation of the rest of my life.
Our desks were at right-angles, so he could see what I was doing. More important for me, I could watch the way he worked.
When I asked him about uncertain points, he was always willing not only to answer the specific question, but to teach me the reasons, the background.
He lent me books, Updike and others . . . . Only later did I realize the reasons for his solutions, always based on a historical background.

Back and front of Puffin Story Book cover designed by Tschichold, 1948. Reduced. Original in full colour.

He was totally uncompromising in maintaining design standards . . .

His craftsmanship was great. I remember that Reynolds Stone had engraved the Shakespeare portrait, in a medallion for the Penguin Shakespeare covers. But Tschichold wanted to make the surrounding border himself. He used scraperboard in actual size, and drew the lettering with a pin held in a pen-holder. He did not need to correct anything: letterspacing, serifs, everything was correct at the first attempt!

All our work was done with the utmost care . . . all our layouts were minutely accurate. We knew that we could never meet the printers, who were scattered all over England. All our communication was by writing. A very few questions were answered by telephone. It forced us to take the utmost trouble with our layouts . . . distance does not matter if your specifications are complete.'

Some of the Penguin symbols drawn by
Tschichold in 1947.

Tschichold used his own talent for drawing and lettering when it was needed. He redrew, or supervised the drawing of, all the symbols used to differentiate the various series, some in alternative versions; and his own calligraphy appeared on various covers, e.g. on the titles of various numbers of *Penguin's Progress*. Whenever fine lettering or calligraphy was reproduced in a Penguin book, Tschichold took especial trouble to see that the quality of the reproduction was as nearly perfect as possible. For example, when he was working on Alfred Fairbank's King Penguin *A Book of Scripts* in 1949, he took special pains with the cover panels of roman capitals taken from Juan de Yciar's Spanish manual of 1547. Since even the best available originals had been printed from battered wood-blocks, he used his pen and brush to restore the letters to the shapes their designer intended, before they were photographed for plate-making. As Paul Standard has remarked, this was with him an act of simple *pietas*[2] – but it was also

[2] Paul Standard: 'Jan Tschichold: Proponent of Asymmetry and Tradition'. *Monotype Newsletter* 81, London, May 1967.

The Pelican cover as redesigned by Tschichold.
The border and rules were printed in blue.

WYN GRIFFITH

The Welsh

This is not a history of the country but a study of the culture and environment of the Welsh people as manifested in their political philosophy, literature, arts and their code of religious and social behaviour.

ONE SHILLING AND SIXPENCE

A PELICAN BOOK

A PELICAN BOOK

A PELICAN BOOK

Prospectus cover designed by Tschichold, 1947, with Pelican symbol drawn by Berthold Wolpe. Reduced. Original in black and terracotta on toned paper.

THE

TO BE PUBLISHED BY

PELICAN

PENGUIN BOOKS LIMITED

HISTORY

HARMONDSWORTH · MIDDLESEX

OF ART

THE PENROSE ANNUAL

REVIEW OF THE GRAPHIC ARTS

EDITED BY R. B. FISHENDEN · M.SC. (TECH.) F.R.P.S.

VOLUME FORTY-THREE

1949

PERCY LUND HUMPHRIES & CO · LTD

TWELVE BEDFORD SQUARE

LONDON WC · I

something else. Every good book designer knows that no pain or trouble is too much to ensure that one's originals are as good as they can possibly be: but not all book designers are also master calligraphers. He also himself drew the small lettering for A BOOK OF SCRIPTS and A KING PENGUIN on the front cover of *A Book of Scripts*, not finding any type-face that was exactly what he wanted; and, as described by Frederiksen, the small lettering in the borders of the Penguin Shakespeare covers. For the cover of a Puffin Picture Book on *Early Man* he dipped his finger in indian ink and wrote the title with his finger tip.

In December 1949, as a result of a heavy devaluation of the pound, Tschichold decided to return to Switzerland: his work of reconstruction at Penguin Books was in any case complete. He had probably done more for British book production as a whole than any other single book designer had ever done. He had not sought to dazzle by a display of personal virtuosity, but he had re-emphasized that incessant carefulness and attention to detail is as important a part of book production as careful editing. In 1949, and for many years afterwards, Tschichold could have echoed Wren in any English bookshop – 'si monumentum requiris, circumspice' – 'if you seek my monument, look around you'. A little later, in 1951, he published a book reproducing many of his best designs for Penguins (and publishers in Switzerland) which gives a splendid conspectus of his work as a book designer. It appeared in German as *Im Dienste des Buches*, St Gallen: SGM–Bücherei; in Danish as *I Bogens Tjeneste*, Copenhagen: Forening for Boghaandvaerk; and in English as *Designing Books*, New York: Wittenborn, Schultz Inc. (no English publisher) – all in 1951.

Symbol for *Typographische Monatsblätter* designed by Tschichold, 1951.

On his return to Switzerland, Tschichold continued to practise as a typographical consultant for various Swiss and German publishers. In 1954 he was invited to become Director of the Munich Academy of Graphic Arts, from which he had been expelled in 1933 and which was now attaining University status. To have accepted this post and returned to live in Germany would have prejudiced his Swiss citizenship so he declined. In 1955 he accepted a post as design consultant to the large pharmaceutical firm of F. Hoffman-La Roche & Co. AG in Basle. He designed their entire and not inconsiderable output of literature, not to mention labels, advertisements and stationery (see pp. 110–11) until 1967. For La Roche booklets, explaining the uses of new drugs to the medical profession, Tschichold used a large format (240 × 160 mm) with ample margins. Most of the books are set in Garamond and printed on toned Basingwerk Parchment, are illustrated with half-tones and line diagrams, and often printed in two or three colours. They are readable and attractive but not over-designed, as is often the case with such industrial literature. He also executed numerous miscellaneous commissions, including posters and ancillary literature for music festivals in the city of Basle and elsewhere.

He continued to write and compile his own books, on a variety of aspects of printing and book design. Perhaps the most important was the *Meisterbuch der Schrift*, published by Otto Maier Verlag, Ravensburg, in 1952, and later published in English as *Treasury of Alphabets and Lettering* by Reinhold, New York, in 1966: it consists of an authoritative introductory essay on letter-forms and typographic principles, followed by 176 pages of plates in half-tone and line, beautifully printed by offset.

Tschichold had always since his earliest days spent a great deal of time in research on all aspects of the history of calligraphy, printing, and book design; and, as

HERMANN
HESSE

DIESSEITS·
KLEINE

WELT·

FABULIER-
BUCH

HERMANN
HESSE
DIESSEITS·
KLEINE
WELT·
FABULIER-
BUCH

Suhrkamp Verlag

Jacket designed by Tschichold, 1954. Original in
black and brown on cream.

Sophie Taeuber-Arp

Cover for Sophie Taeuber-Arp
catalogue, 1954. Original in grey on
light blue.

JAN TSCHICHOLD

FORMENWANDLUNGEN

&

DER ET-ZEICHEN

Cover of a booklet designed by Tschichold, 1954.
Actual size. Original in black and brown on
cream.

A „must"

$4\frac{1}{2}$

Schönste liebe mich

Deutsche Liebesgedichte

aus dem Barock und dem Rokoko

Mit farbigen Wiedergaben

acht alter Spitzenbildchen

$3\frac{1}{2}$

Verlag Lambert Schneider,

Heidelberg

1957.

Jan Tschichold: Title, 1957. Full size.

A specification by
Tschichold, 1957.

Border to be set, 24 by 38 pica ems.
Please observe upper and left-hand margins
as indicated, precisely! Use the same thickness of like
as in upper part of
Do not centre it. Jan Tschichold, Hon. R.D.I. the
CH 6611 BERZONA Onsernone illu-
stration
(Schweiz, Switzerland)

JÜRG BÄR

———

Die

Funktionen

der

Vitamine

VII

Der Bedarf an Vitaminen

Der Vitaminbedarf des Menschen hängt von verschiedenen Faktoren ab und ist nicht von konstanter Größe. Da Kinder einen kleineren Körper als die Erwachsenen mit Vitaminen zu versorgen haben, ist ihr Bedarf in absoluten Zahlen geringer, relativ jedoch ist er größer, denn Wachstum und Entwicklung verlangen eine erhöhte Zufuhr. Das gilt nicht nur für die Vitamine, die an diesen Vorgängen unmittelbar beteiligt sind, sondern auch für die übrigen Vitamine. Ebenso liegt es auf der Hand, daß schwangere und stillende Frauen einen erhöhten Vitaminbedarf haben, da sie ja nicht nur sich selbst, sondern auch noch das herankeimende Lebewesen bzw. den Säugling versorgen müssen. Besonders hohe Dosen, die oft ein Vielfaches des normalen Tagesbedarfes betragen, werden zu therapeutischen Zwecken gegeben. Die Vitaminbehandlung muß von zwei verschiedenen Standpunkten aus betrachtet werden: Sie ist einmal indiziert, wenn Hypovitaminosen oder Avitaminosen vorliegen, das heißt wenn eigentliche Vitamin-Mangelkrank-

261

Cover and text page of booklet designed by Tschichold for Hoffmann-La Roche, 1961. Reduced. Cover printed in black and red on green.

mentioned above, his researches included the history of colour-printing techniques in China. The scholarship that underlay all his designing cannot be over-emphasized. One of his major interests was the considerations underlying the choice of margins throughout the history of the book, both written and printed. On this subject he published *Die Proportionen des Buches* (The proportions of the book), 1956, translated into several languages but never published in England, and an important essay *Willkürfreie Massverhältnisse der Buchseite und des Satzspiegels*, published in England in *Print in Britain*, September 1963, as 'Non-arbitrary proportions of page and type area'. He also compiled a charming anthology of German Baroque love poems, *Schönste, liebe mich*, Heidelberg, 1957, illustrated with reproductions in colour of 'Spitzenbilder', the old German pricked-vellum or paper pictures which he had been collecting for some years.

Cover for booklet for Hoffmann-La Roche, 1965.
Original in yellow and dark green.

Le ‹Valium› Roche
en tant
que myorelaxant

F. HOFFMANN-LA ROCHE & CIE
SOCIÉTÉ ANONYME
BÂLE

Jacket designed by Tschichold, 1961.
Reduced. Original in black and terracotta on
cream.

Jan Tschichold

Geschichte

der

Schrift

in

Bildern

Hauswedell

II.1

Ein offener platz, der an Capulets garten stößt.
Romeo tritt auf.

ROMEO.

Kann ich von hinnen, da mein herz hier bleibt?
Geh, frostge erde, suche deine sonne!
Er ersteigt die mauer und springt hinunter.
Benvolio und Mercutio treten auf.
BENVOLIO. He, Romeo! he, vetter!
MERCUTIO. Er ist klug
Und hat, mein seel, sich heim ins bett gestohlen.
BENVOLIO. Er lief hieher und sprang die gartenmauer
Hinüber. Ruf ihn, freund Mercutio.
MERCUTIO. Ja, auch beschwören will ich. Romeo!
Was? Grillen! Toller! Leidenschaft! Verliebter!
Erscheine du, gestaltet wie ein seufzer;
Sprich nur ein reimchen, so genügt mirs schon;
Ein ach nur jammre, paare lieb und triebe;
Gib der gevattrin Venus Ein gut wort,
Schimpf eins auf ihren blinden sohn und erben,
Held Amor, der so flink gezielt, als könig
Kophetua das bettlermädchen liebte.'
Er höret nicht, er regt sich nicht, er rührt sich nicht.
Der aff ist tot; ich muß ihn wohl beschwören.
Nun wohl: Bei Rosalindens hellem auge,
Bei ihrer purpurlipp und hohen stirn,
Bei ihrem zarten fuß, dem schlanken bein,
Den üppgen hüften und der region,
Die ihnen nahe liegt, beschwör ich dich,
Daß du in eigner bildung uns erscheinest.
BENVOLIO. Wenn er dich hört, so wird er zornig werden.

28

MERCUTIO. Hierüber kann ers nicht; er hätte grund,
Bannt ich hinauf in seiner dame kreis
Ihm einen geist von seltsam eigner art
Und ließe den da stehn, bis sie den trotz
Gezähmt und nieder ihn beschworen hätte.
Das wär beschimpfung! Meine anrufung
Ist gut und ehrlich; mit der liebsten namen
Beschwör ich ihn, bloß um ihn herzubannen.
BENVOLIO. Komm! Er verbarg sich unter jenen bäumen
Und pflegt' des umgangs mit der feuchten nacht.
Die lieb ist blind, das dunkel ist ihr recht.
MERCUTIO. Ist liebe blind, so zielt sie freilich schlecht.
Nun sitzt er wohl an einen baum gelehnt
Und wünscht, sein liebchen wär die reife frucht
Und fiel ihm in den schoß. Doch, gute nacht,
Freund Romeo! Ich will ins federbett;
Das feldbett ist zum schlafen mir zu kalt.
Kommt, gehn wir!
BENVOLIO. Ja, es ist vergeblich, ihn
Zu suchen, der nicht will gefunden sein. *Ab.*

II.2

Capulets garten.
Romeo kommt.

ROMEO.

Der narben lacht, wer wunden nie gefühlt.
Julia erscheint oben an einem fenster.
Doch still, was schimmert durch das fenster dort?
Es ist der ost, und Julia die sonne! —
Geh auf, du holde sonn! ertöte Lunen,

29

Opening of a projected edition of Shakespeare,
designed by Tschichold in Haasscher Caslon,
which won a Gold Medal at the Leipzig
International Book Exhibition, 1964. Reduced.
Original in black with the italic stage directions at
the tops of scenes in red.

In 1960 he published *Erfreuliche Drucksachen durch gute Typographie* (Otto Maier Verlag, Ravensburg), literally, 'Enjoyable printed matter by means of good typography'; an introduction for the general reader to the appreciation of good design in lettering and printing, with excellent illustrations of 'right' and 'wrong' in the shapes of letters and the arrangement of type, margins and illustrations.

Tschichold's last important typographical commission was the creation of 'Sabon', a type-face designed to meet specific technical requirements.

In 1960, a group of German master printers formulated the requirements of a new type-face which they had decided they needed, and commissioned Tschichold to make the drawings for it. The requirements were that it should be suitable for production in identical form for mechanical composition by Linotype and Monotype and for hand composition in foundry types, so that type set by any of the methods would be indistinguishable and interchangeable. In addition, the German group decided that the new type should be easy and pleasant to read and suitable for all printing purposes. They recommended something in the style of Monotype Garamond, but asked for it to be approximately 5% narrower for reasons of economy. The three manufacturing firms were to be the Linotype, Monotype and Stempel companies in Frankfurt.

As John Dreyfus[1] has observed, 'to many type-designers, such a brief would have appeared not merely daunting but dispiriting'; but Tschichold brought to this challenging task his great experience, a deep admiration for the classical type-faces which were to be his model, and all his resources of patience and skill. He made his working drawings, some of which are reproduced here, in a size about twenty times larger than the 10 point size in which the first trial founts were made. The drawings were made expressly for photographic reproduction: no hand punch-cutter was used. The various and considerable technical limitations imposed on the drawing by the requirements of the three manufacturing processes were eventually overcome. 'Sabon' (named after Jacques Sabon, the Lyons-born type founder who worked in Frankfurt and may have bought some of Claude Garamond's matrices in Frankfurt from Garamond's executor) is available in Roman, Italic and Semi-Bold: the Semi-Bold has no Italic, but can be used either in conjunction with the roman, as a normal bold, or independently – where, however, the need for its own Italic might be felt. Sabon is available for film composition by 'Monophoto'.

It is a distinguished addition to the already rich range of book faces available to the modern typographer: whether the requirement for it foreseen by the group of Frankfurt printers actually exists has yet to be discovered. The face itself is really a version of Garamond: its originality lies in the unseen skill with which

[1] John Dreyfus, 'Sabon: the first "harmonized" type', *The Penrose Annual*, London, 1968.

SSAJJA

2. Mai 1965

Der Neuschnitt vom 11.8.65
stimmt nicht mit
dieser Zeichnung
überein. Ist oben
zu breit, und nach
links gedreht.
Endstrich oben rechts
ist ganz anders als
in der Vorlage.
Die Hauptbewegung
ist hier gelähmt.

fl ist in der
Mitte zu
verbinden.
Sonst müßte
man ja auch
fi in der Mitte
trennen!

ft ist unbedingt nötig,
weil wir sonst zu wenig
obere Bogen haben.
Bitte analog dem
fl in der Stärke
korrigieren

chAäek

← hier ist das
normale c. Der Tropfen war
anders. Bitte ck entsprechend
korrigieren

A bleibt
unverändert.

Korrigiert

Korrigiert

Korrigiert

27. 8. 65 Tschichold

Drawings for Sabon, 1965.

Diagrams drawn by Tschichold to illustrate his
theories on proportion and layout using the
Golden Section.

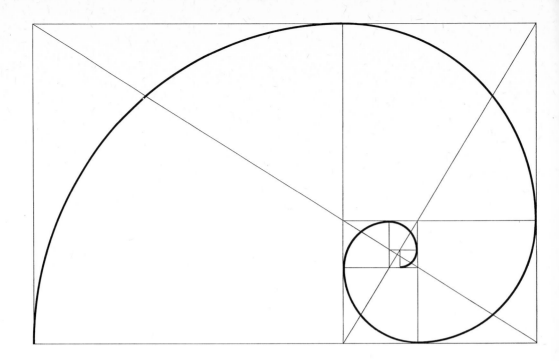

its creator has overcome the technical problems of three sets of body-widths. Its
design is the direct and logical continuation of Tschichold's thinking and
designing of the 1920s: all his career had been devoted to the search for how to
make the fullest use of machine processes to produce humane and logical printing.

Many honours came to Tschichold in the post-war years.

In 1954, he became the first continental European to be awarded the gold medal
of the American Institute of Graphic Arts; and in 1965 the City of Leipzig, on its
800th birthday, awarded him the Gutenberg Prize. In 1965, too, he was
awarded the distinction in London of Honorary Royal Designer for Industry
(HON.RDI), an honour which he much valued. In 1966 he became a Corresponding
Member of the German Academy of Arts in Berlin.

In 1968, the Tschicholds gave up their home in Basle and moved everything to a
house they had previously built and used for holidays, in the village of Berzona,
in Ticino, the southern and Italian-speaking district of Switzerland above
Locarno.

The house had a small but beautiful garden, terraced on the mountain-side, and a
separate apartment, above the garage, designed for their son and his family in
which also visiting friends frequently stayed. In these peaceful surroundings,
Tschichold wrote, designed, and attended to his various collections, which

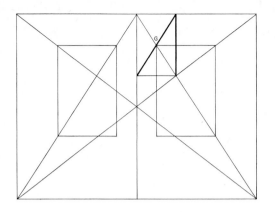 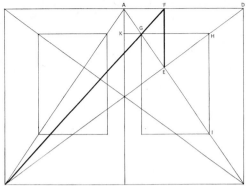 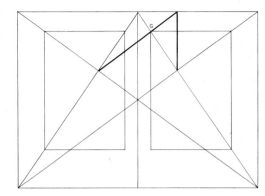

included old engraved trade cards, modern orange papers, all sorts of 'Victoriana' and other items of graphic interest. He had a remarkable collection of early writing books, and also a collection of old paper from which he could find pieces to match a torn page in a writing-book of perhaps, the sixteenth or seventeenth century, and repair it with meticulous and professional skill. In everything he did, his wife supported him with quiet and self-effacing devotion – and with a strong sense of humour.

In the Ticino, the Tschicholds had among their friends and neighbours Max Frisch, Alfred Andersch and Golo Mann, and, in nearby Locarno, the widow of his old friend Hans Arp. They travelled regularly, often to London. Tschichold enjoyed life (although not noise, and hated, for example, shopping in Locarno in the summer). He was narrow only in the sense that he had concentrated every fibre of his being, more even than most artists, in the pursuit of truth in the arts of lettering and typography; he did not paint or draw (outside the practice of lettering and type design) nor did he play any instrument, but he was deeply interested in all the arts, especially painting and sculpture, and read widely. Although like other artists of deep integrity and achievement he took himself and life seriously, he could also smile at himself. He used to relate that a pompous friend from Germany asked him what he had done during the war, to which he replied, 'I was in the Swiss Army' – and when the friend persisted, 'but what *were* you in the Swiss Army' he replied firmly, 'I was a joke in the Swiss Army'.

Poster designed by Tschichold, 1966. Much reduced.

MUSIK-AKADEMIE DER STADT BASEL

Direktion: Dr. h. c. Paul Sacher

Fünf
Orchesterkonzerte
Sommer 1966

23. Juni, 20.15 Uhr im Großen Saal der Musik-Akademie	Manfredini: Konzert D-Dur 2 Trompeten	Haydn: Konzert C-Dur Orgel	Mozart: Exsultate KV 165 Sopran	Joh. Chr. Bach: Symphonie E-Dur	Leitung: Rodolfo Felicani Konservatoriums-Orchester
27. Juni, 20.15 Uhr im Musiksaal des Stadtcasinos	Mozart: Konzert KV 450 Klavier	Mozart: Die Zauberflöte Tenor	Haydn: Die Schöpfung Sopran, Baß	Schönberg: Konzert op. 42 Klavier	Leitung: Erich Schmid Basler Orchestergesellschaft
28. Juni, 20.15 Uhr im Musiksaal des Stadtcasinos	Weber: Konzert op. 11 Klavier	Gluck: Iphigenie in Aulis Sopran	Bennett: Piece for Orchestra	Chopin: Konzert op. 11 Klavier	Leitung: Erich Schmid Basler Orchestergesellschaft
29. Juni, 20.15 Uhr im Musiksaal des Stadtcasinos	Mozart: Konzert KV 459 Klavier	Purcell: Dido und Aeneas Sopran	Bartók: 1. Rhapsodie Violine	Ravel: Konzert G-Dur Klavier	Leitung: Paul Sacher Basler Orchestergesellschaft
30. Juni, 20.15 Uhr im Musiksaal des Stadtcasinos	Beck: Serenade Flöte, Klarinette	Schumann: Konzertstück op. 92 Klavier	Brahms: Konzert op. 77 Violine		Leitung: Joseph Bopp Basler Orchestergesellschaft

JAN TSCHICHOLD

Programme als Eintrittskarten zu 3 Franken
jeweilen eine Woche vor der betreffenden Veranstaltung
bei Hug & Co. und an der Abendkasse

Jan Tschichold **died of cancer** in Locarno Hospital on 11 August 1974. His fundamental contribution to the typography of the twentieth century was made as a teacher of both the broad principles and the narrowest details; he has shown, more clearly than anyone else, that the true task of the typographer is not so much in the broad sweep and the dashing effect, which draws the applause, as in the less obvious, infinitely more difficult and painstaking task of getting *all* the details right – with elegance.

Jan Tschichold in his garden at Berzona, Easter 1968. Photograph taken by the author.

A selected list of books
by Jan Tschichold

Die neue Typographie. Berlin, 1928
foto-auge (with Franz Roh). Stuttgart, 1929
Eine Stunde Druckgestaltung. Stuttgart, 1930
Schriftschreiben für Setzer. Frankfurt am Main, 1931
Typografische Entwurfstechnik. Stuttgart, 1932
Typographische Gestaltung. Basle, 1935
Der frühe chinesische Farbendruck. Basle, 1940
Geschichte der Schrift in Bildern. Basle, 1941
Gute Schriftformen. Basle, 1941–2
Schriftkunde, Schreibübungen und Skizzieren für Setzer. Basle, 1942
Chinesische Farbendrucke der Gegenwart. Basle, 1944
Schatzkammer der Schreibkunst. Basle, 1945
Was jedermann vom Buchdruck wissen sollte. Basle, 1949
Im dienste des Buches. St Gallen, 1951
Meisterbuch der Schrift. Ravensburg, 1952
Formenwandlungen der & Zeichen. Frankfurt am Main, 1954
Die Proportionen des Buches. Stuttgart, 1955
Schönste, liebe mich. Heidelberg, 1957
Der Chinesische und der japanische mehrfarbige Holztafeldruck, technisch. Basle, 1959
Erfreuliche Drucksachen durch gute Typographie. Ravensburg, 1960
Zur Typographie der Gegenwart. Bern, 1960
Die Bildersammlung der Zehnbambushalle. Erlenbach, 1970
Ausgewählte Aufsätze über Fragen der Gestalt des Buches und der Typographie. Basle, 1975

Works by Jan Tschichold published in English translation

Early Chinese Colour Printing. London and New York, 1940
Chinese Colour Printing of the present day. London and New York, 1953
An Illustrated History of Lettering and Writing. London, 1947
About Calligraphy, Typography and Letterspacing. Southampton College of Art, 1951
Designing Books. New York, 1951
Contemporary Typography. The New Laboratory Press. Pittsburgh, 1961
Treasury of Alphabets and Lettering. New York, 1966
Asymmetric Typography. London and New York, 1967
Chinese Colour Prints from the Ten Bamboo Studio. London and New York, 1972
John Seddon: The Penman's Paradise. Cantz, Stuttgart, 1966

Appendices

Appendix 1 : The placing of type in a given space

Die Anordnung des Schriftsatzes in Flächenraum
Typographische Monatsblätter, No.7, 1934

It is not enough to know exactly how words, lines and paragraphs should be set. One must also know how to place the type in the space available.

Let us deal first with a simple problem: the relationship of a heading to a paragraph and their joint relationship to the space.

The old way of positioning a heading is to centre it: this is *centred typography*. This is comparatively simple and presents no great difficulties (Example 1). (But not all compositors know how to design centred typography, although it has been practised for centuries.) Text and headings are exactly centred. The top margin may be of exactly the same width as the side margins or may be of a different width; but the bottom margin must nearly always be distinctly wider than all the others. The heading must be shorter than the width of the text. If it is longer, or of the same width, it must be broken. In this traditional style of setting, the heading is usually set in larger type rather than in bolder.

Let us now, using the same setting, arrange it differently in the space available. For our present purposes, 'space' means the trimmed page or the space enclosed within rules in an advertisement, etc.

Let us try moving the heading to one side (Example 2). If we do this, the design loses the balance that it had before. The setting looks lop-sided. *In general, asymmetrical type matter should not be placed centrally*. So we must restore the balance (Example 3). The result is surprising: but it is not pleasing. We read from left to right and we therefore need space for the eye to pick up each line that it has to read, which now we have not got. Nor is the heading well placed. But first let us try to find a better position for the main text (Example 4).

This layout too has its faults. Yet the eye can pick up the lines better than before. The type area, however, has been pushed too far to the right. (It should be said here that in this and similar cases the right-hand margin should be at least a little wider than the space between words.) If we compare the width of the space to the left of the type area (a) with the width of the type area (b) the slight difference is displeasing. We can eliminate it and at the same time avoid pushing the type area too far to the right if we shift it some of the way back to the left (Example 5).

The balance is now restored. Our experiment leads to the conclusion that it is usually *better to move the type area from the centre to the right rather than to the left*. (In Hebrew and Chinese, where the writing runs in the reverse direction, it would be necessary to adopt the opposite course.)

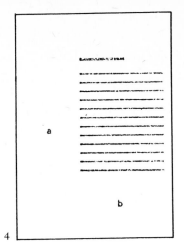

Yet our layout can be improved even further. It looks better if it is placed a little higher (Example 6). The heading looks better if it is moved up a little, for this makes the page look less ponderous and relates the type area better to the space (Example 7). In order to avoid the rigidity of Example 5 we could (Example 8) give the heading the same indentation as the paragraphs of the text, say 12 points. Em indentations are still the best means of indicating paragraphs and are not at all 'old-fashioned'. But this makes the design rather weak. It can only be improved by an unusually strong indentation (Example 9). Let us therefore try indenting the main text the same amount as the heading (Example 10). This is better on the whole. But the heading is now very prominent and calls for a counterweight at the bottom. If we cannot make one (a page-number, for example) we must give up the idea of putting the heading in this position. However, the solutions 6, 7, 9 and 10 are not the only possibilities. We can move the type area, for example, even higher and move the heading further away. Even the smallest change gives a new look. The layout can be made to look different by further increasing the indentation, by putting more space between two paragraphs, etc.

We must ask ourselves each time whether the result is *pleasing*, whether we have achieved a balance. Provided the work is all right technically, there is no other criterion for typographical design.

Even if some students do not start out with a sure feeling for the design of a printed page, it can still be learned and taught. Continual critical study of good work is the best way to achieve this.

The choice of type for the heading of a piece of plain text is far less complicated than the *choice of sizes* for an average piece of jobbing composition. We should as a rule use *as few sizes as possible*; but three are usually the fewest that can be used

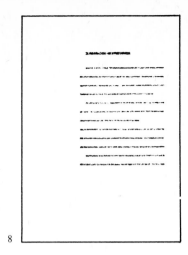

successfully. Between three and five should almost always be enough, although more can be used occasionally. In any case, the number of sizes is by no means all that matters. The relationship between the sizes is much more important. All relationships of this kind should be distinct and clear and those that are not should be avoided (for example, 9 should not be used with 10-point, or 14 with 16-point).

Printers used to use only one type-face, and set the title in a larger size of it. Most printers today prefer the more lively contrast of ordinary and bold, in which they can stick to one size. The relationship of the sizes must in any case be clearly visible, its effect must be lively and it must always follow the sense of the text exactly.

A printing job is seldom as simple as the little diagrams at the beginning of this article. If we re-examine the results of our enquiries into the placing of type on the page, we shall quickly see that the margins have an extremely important bearing on the effect of the layout. We ended by making all the margins unequal. The compositor must always consider the white space in his layouts. Each line of his text is separated from the others by an amount of white space. On the one hand the amount of white is subject to logical and technical considerations (sense of the lines, their context; space available); on the other, the areas of white determine to a very great extent the artistic effect of the whole. In my book *Typographische Entwurfstechnik* I have argued that these areas of white should always be unequal. The inequality must, of course, follow the sense and continuity of the text. But the areas of white must also be harmonious and must really help to create the total effect. In a piece of good typographical design even the smallest element has its significance. Areas of white can have two possible relationships with each other: they can be equal or unequal. Unequal margins break the monotony of the solid type. A page with exactly equal margins looks dull. Large and small areas of white, if they can be compared, must be clearly differentiated: too small a difference is unpleasing. One good relationship is the often despised and often unnecessarily advocated Golden Section. It is, however, only *one* relationship. We must not allow ourselves to be guided initially by these proportions, but by feeling first of all, and only at the end should we examine the proportions of the work and the possibility of improving them. To divide up the space blindly according to the Golden Section is wrong and just as harmful to the general effect as, for example, setting type in arbitrary shapes. The division must first of all follow the requirements of the text and its meaning.

The areas of white in a well-designed piece of work are not only graduated and unequal but are *rhythmically unequal*. A closer look at the illustrations to this article will show several possibilities, which are always different in every job. We should look not only at the white space created by the leading but also at the measures. The relative sizes and the relationships between the headings and the text – today often enlivened by the use of semi-bold – are every bit as important.

The greatest benefit from looking at good work will always be gained by those who study its finest details and subtleties. This is the only way to teach oneself typographic design.

Appendix 2 : The design of centred typography

Vom richtigen Satz auf Mittelachse
Typographische Monatsblätter, No.4, 1935

The practice of centering headings and titles came in soon after the invention of printing: the possibility of centering words is inherent in the nature of movable type. The printer, unlike the scribe, can move the individual words of a title, once they have been set, wherever he likes. What is easy for the printer requires considerable skill from the scribe. But centred arrangements also harmonized with the style of the dawning Renaissance, which, in general, raised centred design to become the artistic norm (cf. Leonardo's *Last Supper*). That the central axis in typography has persisted until quite recently is due in the main to the prevailing styles of art, which typography, like every other sphere of artistic creation, usually follows. Baroque and Rococo had little influence on typographical design; they never questioned the principle of axial setting. Nor did the styles of the Empire, Biedermeier, Second Empire or the style of the *Gründerjahre* (1870–80). Not until the period after 1880, in particular that of the *Freie Richtung* (*c.*1890) and later the *Jugendstil* (1900–8), was asymmetrical setting occasionally tried out. It was not so much technical as aesthetic considerations that led to the posing of new problems, questions concerning the *appearance* of the printed page. People had grown tired of the everlasting sameness and demanded eccentric instead of symmetrical design. Certain works of this period are the forerunners of the new asymmetrical setting that emerged after the First World War. Above all, however, they are the forerunners of a new attitude to form in all spheres that no longer acknowledges the norms of a Renaissance that has continued for 450 years.

The revolution in ideas on form is most clearly apparent in the prodigious development of painting over the past fifty years; the only parallel to this is in the development in the understanding of physics that has taken place quite recently; and unfortunately neither yet comes anywhere near to forming part of our general education. It can be shown that painting, especially after Cubism (1910), had an unprecedented effect in areas that it had not previously influenced, especially architecture and industrial design. People say that architecture today is again supreme among the arts, but they forget that the new architecture would not exist without Cubism (Picasso among others) and abstract painting (especially Mondrian and the Neo-Plastic artists). Among the arts of the present day, therefore, painting, more specifically the work of the abstract artists, is intellectually paramount. These painters have also strongly, if for the most part indirectly, influenced the typography of the present day.

Why then is most typography of today centred? Some subjects by their very nature do no suit an explicitly modern style of typography; it runs contrary to them. Since we must uphold the principle of identity between content and expression, there is no excuse for clothing every theme in modern dress. But all work of a contemporary character (such as contemporary house-building, contemporary opinion, fashion, etc.) should be designed in a modern style. Just as it would appear absurd to put such work in historical dress, a sensitive individual finds it disturbing when things are presented in a typographical form that has nothing in common with the things themselves. That oldest and simplest method of naming a firm followed by a list of its products also has a certain influence on form. In such advertisements a centred design is not only intellectually appropriate, but also offers advantages in setting, since short and very short lines look better when centred. (Asymmetrical design demands strong horizontal groups, i.e. lines of several words.) This now rather old-fashioned style of setting is the exact opposite of the sophisticated American advertisements, with which everybody is familiar from car advertisement if from nothing else, and which results automatically in asymmetrical composition. Finally, there are items that are often impossible to put into a new form and can only be done symmetrically. Even when we are trying to get a quart into a pint pot, as is often required, the symmetrical solution is still often the most elegant.

These few but important reasons alone require that every compositor should still be able to set up an ordinary symmetrical page. And it is probably impossible to set up a good asymmetrical page if you cannot even produce a symmetrical one.

From the *formal* point of view, symmetrical setting is easier and more convenient than modern setting, the advantage of which lies rather in *technical* convenience. There are, however, not many compositors who can produce really good symmetrical setting. It is an art, or can be an art. (But it is not the art of the present day!) Therefore every compositor who values all-round ability must try to familiarize himself with the working rules of good symmetrical design. His mastery of the rules will show most clearly in a symmetrical title-page. I list the principal rules for setting a symmetrical title in Roman type:

The type-face and size of type for the title should be the same as the text face of the book;

Ordinary type (lower case and capitals) must never be letter-spaced. (Words in *Fraktur* may be letter-spaced.)

The most important lines should be set in capitals. In special cases the whole title may be set in capitals, but then the smallest size used must be one size smaller than the basic type of the book. *Here as always capitals* must be *carefully letter-spaced*. Lines of unspaced capitals are always bad, despite the fact that, regrettably, even type-founders have recently begun to present lines of unspaced capitals in their specimens. We can lay it down as a rule that capitals should normally be letter-spaced to between a fifth and a sixth of the point size. Naturally the optical effect of the space between letters must be 'equalized'. This needs to be repeated over and over again, for it is all too rarely observed.

Words like 'by', 'of', etc. may be given a line to themselves, though there are cases in which this is unnecessary. These words need not be set in a smaller type than the following lines. Anyway, the choice and gradation of sizes must correspond to the different values of the words. As a rule more than four sizes on a title-page are bad.

If the capitals are letter-spaced strictly according to the above rule and if lower case lines are not letter-spaced (and word spacing is even, about middle spaces throughout) the result will be lines of unequal length. The structure of the title must be further developed out of these *lines of unequal length*. It is axiomatic that *lines of equal length* (which are not easily obtainable in any case) should be regarded as *unbeautiful*. So, in a symmetrically set title: *never allow lines of equal length*. If lines turn out to be of equal length they must be further justified to make them slightly unequal. At the same time care must be taken to achieve good groupings of lines or at any rate to avoid bad ones. The following are good groupings:

a   b   c

these are bad groupings:

e   f   g

(if at the head)   (if at the foot)

Grouping c can be transformed by a short line below it into grouping a (the 'ideal line-grouping'). The group of lines must, however, not merely look right, the word-groups must also seem to divide naturally. Therefore,

Bridal Bouquets and
Table Decorations in a Wide Range of Prices

———

Telephone 41 406

is wrong, since the 'and' belongs more to 'Table Decorations'.
When speaking slowly we make the division *before* the 'and'. It would therefore be more correct to break thus:

Bridal Bouquets and Table Decorations
in a Wide Range of Prices

—————

Telephone 41 406

or

Bridal Bouquets
and Table Decorations
in a Wide Range of Prices

———

Telephone 41 406

Question: Why is the rule in the middle example longer than in the others?

Only one or at most two rules should be used in a title; they should be of unequal lengths. One often sees a rule in the lower part, near the imprint. If there is a line at the top of the same length or of the width of the type area, the rule below should be between two and four ems shorter than the principal line, since a line always looks shorter than a rule that is not in closest proximity to it. It is better, however, not to use any such rule.

On the question of the grouping of a title, it remains to be said that in order to achieve greater clarity of design the groups must always be the obvious ones. More than two groups are bad. A simple title comprises two groups; one is at the top, the other at the foot of the type area (example a). Example b must appear unbeautiful, even though it is quite often seen.

A title must not be broader and taller than the type area, but may well be narrower and sometimes shorter; and it must be placed in the exact centre of the normal type area. It must therefore not be allowed to assume a 'sovereign' position on the paper; thus it must not, for example, be placed in the centre of the paper. The blank page opposite would make it appear to have been pushed too far to the right.

The form of a title as a whole is thus dependent on many particulars, first and foremost on the text. Yet its form must be pleasing and all this is not so simple. The matter does not end with setting the title centrally. The publication of old title-pages, as this journal has often thought fit to do, is extremely helpful to learners (and who has learnt everything?); from them relationships of size, the fall of the lines and the grouping can be studied in the best way. It should not be thought that these have nothing to do with present-day typography. Time and again the most splendid examples turn out to be Bodoni's title-pages; they contain a wealth of accomplishment that can only be discovered by using them as models.

It is quite rightly said that a title-page is the touchstone of the jobbing printer. The man who can set up a title-page is master of almost all the other fields of setting. At all events, most of what has been said above about the title, the manner of setting it and the fall of the lines applies to other printed work on the axial pattern. We should remember here the old rule that a single-line heading should never be as wide as the solid text below it. This rule, though often transgressed, is still absolutely correct today. What has been said above about the avoidance of 'block setting' obviously does not apply to longer solidly set paragraphs: five or six connected lines of the same length are not 'block setting'.

Advertisements may be set within suitable borders. In symmetrical typography a border can be used like a rich frame made to suit the text within it: in asymmetrical setting this would be stylistically wrong, and one would use only plain rules of varying weight. The space between type area and paper edge must, of course, be the same on the right and left and similar to this space at the top and bottom. Borders can be made of combinations of all varieties of rule.

Here also it is almost always advisable to group or condense the lines into up to three groups; but a more open arrangement is also possible.

In all symmetrical printing, including title-pages, the centre may sometimes be marked by a tiny ornament, a star or a swelled rule. It should be noted, however, that swelled rules can be used only with the following type-faces:

with all Roman faces of French character, such as Bodoni, Didot, Walbaum, French Roman, ordinary Roman, Aldine and similar;
with all classical *Frakturs,* i.e. Lutheran *Fraktur,* Breitkopf, Unger, Walbaum.

Thus the swelled rule is not suited to the *Medieval* Roman (e.g. Garamond), nor to the sans serif types. It is suited only to such faces as have an element of what one might call 'engraving' about them.

It is almost impossible to give further rules for other kinds of symmetrical printing. Nor is there any sense in forcing the whole of typography into a system of rules. The experienced may break the rules from time to time; the beginner must take care to follow the rules where they apply. Thus little by little he will gain the qualities that will permit him one day to break the rules with elegance. Even in symmetrical setting the study of good printing is one of the best methods of self-education.

Appendix 3 : Belief and Reality

Glaube und Wirklichkeit
Schweizer Graphische Mitteilungen, June, 1946

[This article was Tschichold's reply to a savage attack on him by Max Bill on the subject of the 'New Typography'.]

The article, 'on typography', by the Zurich painter and architect Max Bill in the last number [of *Schweizer Graphische Mitteilungen*] seems to have been triggered off by my lecture 'Constants in Typography', delivered last December to the Zurich members of the Association of Swiss Graphic Designers. In this lecture I criticized the 'New Typography' which I helped to disseminate – and therefore myself also – severely. Bill was not among my listeners. The half-understood, grossly distorted quotations from my lecture must have come from second or third hand. Without having informed himself at the source, Bill used this misinformation for a fanatical attack on book typography as practised by myself, Imre Reiner and others.

What I actually said (to quote correctly the words Bill put in my mouth) was: 'The New Typography has indeed not yet been superseded, but it has proved itself to be suitable only for advertising and jobbing. For the book, and particularly for literature, it is completely unsuitable.' I still stand by my textbook, *Typographische Gestaltung* (Basle: Benno Schwabe & Co., 1935). I would change scarcely a word of it, but in a new edition I would delete the final chapter on book typography.

Since my 'threadbare' and 'reactionary' arguments may interest the readers of this magazine, I would like to present them here, without fear that they may 'cause mischief'. I am not, by the way, one of the 'well-known typographical theorists', but, to the best of my knowledge, the only one in German-speaking Europe.

Imre Reiner would probably protest against such a title for himself; he is a fertile and provocative source of ideas rather than a theorist. But I am not merely a theorist, as Bill in fact is; I can look back on more than twenty years' experience as a typographical designer. From 1920–5 I taught lettering at the Academy for Graphic Arts in Leipzig; I also taught typography and lettering for seven years at the Munich Master Printers' School and have been employed ever since coming to Basle in 1933 as designer to two large printing firms. From 1919 until now I have designed not only innumerable pieces of advertising and other printed matter but also hundreds of books of every kind. This extensive practical work and the experience it has brought give my words a different weight from that of the theories of an architect from outside the trade who describes himself as 'more interested in the features of the style periods' and who has only occasionally concerned himself, as an amateur, with typography. He believes himself capable of 'tackling without prejudice problems that grow out of the typographic materials, their requirements and their design', words which, by the way, do not make sense.

The younger generation of compositors cannot easily imagine the condition of German (and Swiss) typography around 1923, before the advent of the New Typography. The average display advertisement and printed job used a variety of type-faces inconceivable today and was uninhibited by any rules of order. The New Typography, disseminated mainly by a number of the *Typographische Mitteilungen* (Leipzig 1925) which I edited and my book of the same name (Berlin 1928) attempted a clean-up by returning to the simplest forms and rules. We saw aesthetic models in industrial products and, believing the sans serif to be the simplest type-face (wrongly, as it turned out), we declared it to be *the* modern face. At the same time we, a group of artists, attempted to use asymmetry to oust symmetrical design, which was hardly ever employed in an intelligible manner. Everything symmetrical was unthinkingly assigned to the propaganda methods of political absolutism and declared obsolete. The historical value of these efforts toward a typographical upheaval derives from the removal of dead elements from typography, the acceptance of photography, the modernization of typographical rules and many other new stimuli, without which the appearance of today's typography in German-speaking countries would not have been possible. The tragedy was that this truly ascetic simplicity soon reached a point where no further development was possible. It was a recruiting camp for newer developments, needed at the time, but to which no one wanted to return.

The derivation of typographical rules from the principles of painting formerly known as 'abstract' or 'non-objective' and now called 'concrete' (Lissitzky, Mondrian, Moholy-Nagy) resulted in a valuable and temporarily novel typography. But it seems to me no coincidence that this typography was practised almost exclusively in Germany and found little acceptance in other countries. *Because its impatient attitude conforms to the German bent for the absolute, and its military will to regulate and its claim to absolute power reflect those fearful components of the German character which set loose Hitler's power and the Second World War.*

I saw this only later, in democratic Switzerland. Since then I have ceased publicizing the New Typography. The creators of the New Typography were, like myself, most vehement enemies of Nazism (only two, Prof. M.B., Essen, and Dr W.D., Jena, went over to it). At the beginning of the so-called Third Reich my wife and I were taken into 'protective custody' for an extended period, i.e. we were thrown into prison and I lost my teaching position in Munich. Since freedom of thought and work for me come before everything else, I left my homeland and moved to Basle.

For we considered ourselves pioneers of 'progress' and wanted nothing to do with such obviously reactionary things as Hitler planned. When the Hitler 'culture' called us 'cultural Bolsheviks' and called the works of like-minded painters 'degenerate', it was using the same obfuscating, falsifying methods here as everywhere else. The Third Reich was second to none in accelerating technical 'progress' in its war preparations while hypocritically concealing it behind propaganda for medieval forms of society and expression. And since deception was its basis, it could not bear the genuine modernists who, although political opponents, were nevertheless unwittingly not so very far from the delusion of 'order' that ruled the Third Reich. The role of leader that fell to me as the only specialist of the group was itself a 'Führer' role, signifying, as it did, an intellectual guardianship of 'followers' typical of dictator states.

The New or functional Typography is well suited for publicizing industrial products (it has the same origin), and it fulfils that purpose now as well as then. Yet its means of expression are limited because it strives solely for puritanical 'clarity' and 'purity'. This changed only *circa* 1930 when seriffed types were accepted as permissible means of expression. It became clear that only types of the nineteenth century could be used; I finally discovered that the New Typography was actually nothing more than the fulfilment of what the progress-happy nineteenth century had been striving for. And in the type-mixtures of the later New Typography, only the types of the nineteenth century could be used. Bodoni was the forerunner of the New Typography insofar as he undertook to purge roman type of all traces of the original written form and – fortunately less radical than some of his recent twentieth-century disciples – to reconstruct it from the simplest possible geometrical elements.

But there are many typographical problems which cannot be solved on such regimented lines without doing violence to the text. Every experienced typographer knows this. Many jobs, especially books, are far too complicated for the simplifying procedures of the New Typography. And the extremely personal nature of the New Typography presents grave dangers to the coherence of a work when the designer cannot continually check each page and deal with all the minute problems that arise. For it has been shown that the apparently simple rules of functional typography are not common knowledge, because they spring from a special, in effect fanatical, attitude of conspirators into whose group one must first be 'initiated'. Traditional typography is quite different: it is far from being unorganic, it can easily be understood by everybody, its finer points are not difficult to appreciate, it presumes no sectarianism and its application in the hands of a beginner does not produce nearly so many blunders as the New Typography in the hands of the uninitiated.

Bill's present-day typography is marked, like my own work between 1924–35, by a naïve worship of so-called technical progress. The designer who works in this manner values the mechanical production of consumer goods – a characteristic of our times – too highly. We cannot escape manufacturing and using such goods, but we need not place halos over them, just because they come off the conveyor belt assembled with the latest 'efficient' methods.

The machine can do everything. It has no law of its own and cannot shape anything by itself. Its products are given form by man, by the designer's will, even when he believes himself to be 'obeying its laws' and that his 'objective' and unornamented designs are 'impersonal'. The work of a one-hundred-percent 'modern' designer is far more individualistic than items produced unambitiously, anonymously, unthinkingly – which must not prevent us from recognizing a product to be good of its kind and preferring it when it serves its purpose as well as another. But the non-artist does not care in the least if the manufacture of his typewriter or whatever called for a minimum of production time or if the hydraulic press was overloaded. He does not even care if the workers are justly paid, a matter that actually should be of concern to him. He asks only that the typewriter be usable and is happy if it is also cheap.

An artist like Bill probably does not realize what a price in blood and tears the use of efficient production methods has cost 'civilized' humanity and every single worker. For these new machines give Bill or another designer time to play but not to the worker, who, day in and day out, has to tighten the same screw. Since his job cannot satisfy him, this worker seeks relaxation in sports on Sunday and with his stamp collection or some other hobby in the evenings. How different for, say, a gardener, whose work satisfies him and who probably does not think of 'relaxing' at the cinema. Proudly, though here and there quite wrongly, Bill notes in his captions that his examples were machine-set. He forgets that the hand compositor, who must make up and complete the work of the keyboarder, has nowhere near the satisfaction from his work that his grandfather could have found in it. Since he always handles type already set, he cannot finish his day with a feeling of having completed a job by himself.

For the worker, mechanization has thus taken a heavy, almost deadly toll of his meaningful work experiences, and it is simply out of place to set it on a pedestal. That mechanization is 'modern' does not mean that it is also valuable or even good; more likely it is not good. But since we cannot go on without it, we must simply accept it as a condition and not worship it because of its origin!

An ugly telephone bothers an aesthetically oriented person like Bill or myself, but we should not then think that a properly designed telephone is a work of art, or a symbol of it. It is only an instrument, like a hammer – nothing more. It is only what we can do with it that is of value.

The telephone has only recently reached its more or less final form. There are many such things which have been invented within our lifetime and which carry the stamp of engineered industrial production methods. Their forms, the car's for instance, have experienced a rapid development and are no doubt a testimony to our time, although by themselves they may well be without value. The most modern products of our 'culture' are the 'V' weapons and the atom bomb. These are already on the way to determining our way of life and will certainly affect our future.

Believers in progress think they must now reform old things in the spirit of the new. Among them are those which can be changed because their technical character has changed, like the lamp. To make an electric lamp that looks like an old-fashioned oil lamp is nonsense. But apart from this, there are things that have long since reached perfection in form: the riding saddle, scissors, the button.

The book, too, completed its development long ago. Except for foxed paper, occasional poor presswork and a different orthography, a 150-year-old book is just as 'practical' as a new one. Indeed, a book today is seldom so well made. Its format is often less practical and it is composed with less taste and affection. Today's poets can consider themselves lucky when their works are anywhere near as well printed as those of their eighteenth-century colleagues. The observance of typographic rules which have taken centuries to form is no more being eclectic or history-bound than the use by a machine manufacturer of another engineer's patent. On the other hand, it is typical of immaturity to want to dump old rules overboard. One must not – heaven forbid! – follow the herd; one must abandon outworn conventions, be 'modern' and go it alone. Anyone is free to act in this way – but at his own risk.

Bill has designed a small number of books and catalogues. Almost without exception they belong to the fields of the new architecture and the new 'concrete' painting. It is absolutely correct to derive the typographic style of such works from the rules of concrete painting, just as it would be correct to follow baroque typography in a book of baroque poems. Both architecture and typography are applied arts. It is gratifying and right that here and there the photographically illustrated book has developed a style of its own, since the photograph forms a new element posing new design problems. Magazines, too, can be laid out in this style. The attractive magazine *Du*, for example, maintains the best tradition of the New Typography without following Bill's overly strict dogma. I have myself, long before Bill, designed a number of catalogues in the New Typography style which even today I consider suitable, but not exclusively so (cf. the Basle Gewerbemuseum catalogue on type-faces, *Die Schrift*).

All of Bill's books show great feeling for form and a sure taste; of their kind they are exemplary. But when Bill teaches that this style is suitable for every other sort of book he shows either a lack of understanding for books whose content is not familiar to him or a dogmatic obstinacy. Other than Bill and a certain Basle sociologist, no one believes that. Novelty and a surprising form are tolerable only in a small group of books; in most others they are disturbing and obtrusive.

Obeying good rules of composition and book design in the manner of traditional typography is not 'putting the clock back'; but an eccentric style of setting is almost always debatable. Thus, the layout of Bill's article is exciting because unusual, but is not to be taken as a model for general imitation. I mention parenthetically that the ragged-right setting Bill uses was first introduced about 1930 by Eric Gill, the great English type designer, and has less point in machine than in hand composition. (For while the hand compositor must take trouble to justify lines evenly, the machine takes care of this automatically and quite well, except for a few faults that only the hand compositor can avoid.) So it is only an apparent simplification and apparently modern in form.

Much more dangerous is Bill's lack of indentations. He marks paragraphs by extra space. Not only does this produce big gaps in the text, but more importantly, it does not guarantee the recognition of new paragraphs, especially at the beginning of a new page (as occurs on page eight of Bill's article). For more on indenting, see my article in the February (1946) issue of *Schweizer Graphische Mitteilungen*.

To show that a Chinese classic in a European language is better when set in our traditional typography, I illustrate a page from Chung T'si, and next to it the continuation in the New Typography. *Exempla docent.* That not every title-page can be set in the empty manner of the New or functional Typography is shown in *Hafis*, a collection of Persian poems, and the facing illustration. The art of the book demands, above all, tact and imagination.

Even the choice of Bodoni for the 'functional' *Hafis* title-page may to Bill appear to be a compromise, because he holds the sans serif to be still the best, the 'up-to-date' type-face. But reading long pages set in it is genuine torture, as is graphically shown in the unreduced reproduction from a book that actually appeared (Berne 1942).

The sans is not a new face, having appeared in the first third of the nineteenth century. It is primarily useful for titles and only short paragraphs of text, since its lack of sufficient articulation and indispensable serifs, together with unvarying stroke weights, make it difficult to read. It is simple only at first glance and corresponds rather to the undeveloped perceptions of children learning to spell and to whose unpractised eye the genuine letter forms of printing types appear as complicated as the handwriting of a twelve-year-old schoolgirl.

It is no coincidence that most followers of the functional typography want to know little or nothing of the better sans serif formulations of today's type designers (Eric Gill's Sans, W. A. Dwiggins's Metro). These show the true calligraphy of the present day and tower above the deplorable level of the common sans serifs (Akzidenz-Grotesk, Monotype Series 215) which Bill likes to use.

The best, most legible types that are available to us are the classic faces (e.g. Bembo, Garamond, Ehrhardt, Van Dijck, Caslon, Bell, Baskerville, Walbaum) and those new ones that differ but little from them (Perpetua, Lutetia, Romulus and several others). That faces of both kinds are available today is the special achievement of Stanley Morison during twenty-five years' activity with a leading English firm. The rebirth of the classic types brought with it a typographic revival the world over that is at least as important as the cleaning-up process of the New Typography was for Germany.

But the technical principle of machine composition has not had the least influence on typographical design methods. Machine composition imitates hand composition, the nearer the better; if it had other than optical aims, such as mere technical expediency, it would come close to the unusable, optically inadequate compromise of a typewriter type. Machine composition is neither cheaper

(Switzerland 1946) nor better than hand composition except for the newly cast printing surface it produces; it is less flexible and not at all easier to handle than hand composition. It is more efficient but in no way able to change materially the appearance of typography by means of some sort of 'mechanical' law of its own. Bill cannot himself recognize machine composition; not everything he claims ought to be, or could be, set by machine is in fact so. For the good keyboarder, like the hand compositor, strives for optical perfection, a perfection which was reached as early as the sixteenth century and has not been bettered since. Further, the limitations of certain typesetting-machine systems have produced bothersome letter forms that disturb the educated eye, while types for hand composition allow, thanks to their unlimited number of set widths, the ultimate in optical finesse. This is far more important than Bill, a layman, realizes.

Unlike the book, promotional printing has developed in our own time, a true child of the industrial age. Since advertising requires novelty and surprise, the New Typography with its new forms enjoyed favour for a time – as long as it was still 'new'. But when its ascetic character was well enough known, the search for other new forms began, some of which naturally tended to the other extreme of ornamental typography. This can also have a refreshing effect, like a flower in rocky terrain. It would be wrong to see ornamental typography, incidentally only occasionally suitable, as *the* modern form; both are modern if one refrains from investing the word 'modern' with value judgments. It does not signify 'novel' or 'new' but rather that something was produced today, not twenty or a hundred years ago, and that things – good or bad – are now manufactured that way.

Since nothing new remains new forever, the appearance of typography will continue to change, perhaps to the point where today's competitive economic system will have to give way to one based merely on what is needed. He who does away with surprise, the goal that puritanical, functional typography aims for, and would like to limit himself to a sober presentation of the message, will learn a lesson when he has to fulfil the sometimes unreasonable wishes of his customers. It is a notable deficiency of the New or functional Typography that it is not suitable for work which must reflect the character of an institution. It is forced to extreme solutions which are often far from 'practical' (e.g. use of several colours, superfluous halftones, expensive paper).

The lasting contributions of the New Typography are tight setting, better composition, better type-faces and the dissemination of useful rules, which Bill disapprovingly calls recipes. If one takes the trouble to sift them from my writings, these rules emerge:

1. Fewest possible type-faces.
2. Fewest possible type sizes.
3. No letter-spacing of lower case [still encountered in German-speaking countries today, mainly in provincial newspapers].
4. Emphasis by using italic or bold of the same face.
5. Use capitals only as an exception, then always carefully letter-spaced.
6. Form groups – not more than three.

Bill himself does not realize how faithfully he follows these 'recipes' of mine: I could cite nearly all his typographical works as examples of their correct use. It is obvious that not everyone who obeys reasonable rules can be a good designer. There will always be bad imitators. I can no more be held responsible for my imitators than I hold Bill responsible for his.

I am no friend of a parochial 'olde worlde' style; the traditional typography that I defend here is not that, though something similar probably still exists. Even in Germany we called the efforts of Rudolf Koch and his followers the 'national wildlife sanctuary'. Ending with Marathon (Koch Klingspor 1931), the 'sanctuary' harboured Post-Antiqua and Post-Fraktur and, three degrees below it, the bastard gothic types of the Third Reich (Tannenberg, Deutschland, National). I cannot stand these types. They spring from a reversal of the quasi-religious belief in progress, such as Bill stands for, a sentimental flight into an irretrievable past. (These types are, by the way, also 'modern'.)

If the newly revived traditional typography were the outcome of Nazi propaganda, such as Bill dares to claim, the typography of the whole world, Russia included, would have been influenced by it decades ago. I practise and preach a typography which, good or bad, is used everywhere. For I believe it is a waste of time to set on a pedestal one stage of a typographical renovation process, such as German typography was going through around 1930.

Bill hints that he has been defamed. Nothing could be farther from my intention. I cannot believe that in my lecture I mentioned Bill's name or work, which, as explained above, I accept unreservedly. Indeed, I have taken my own earlier work, not his, to task. What bothers me most is that he seems to deny me the right to work in the way I find best. As an artist he must know that a creative person can only work in the way he believes right. *He who calls for the suppression of freedom of thought and artistic expression carries on the gloomy business of those whom we thought were defeated. He commits the worst crime, for he buries our highest good, the sign of man's worth – freedom.* Which perhaps a man must first lose, as I did, before he can discover its true value.

Appendix 4: On mass-producing the classics

Signature, No.3 (New Series), March, 1947

If an ordinary book deserves to be produced with the greatest possible care, then, certainly, so does a classic. The word 'classic' is perhaps too freely used nowadays, and is indeed applied to many more books than would have been the case fifty years ago. But all books whose value has been proved to be lasting deserve to be produced worthily: not only in spite of the fact that they have to be produced in such large numbers, but because of it. And faultless typography costs no more for a huge edition than for a limited one. Publishers indeed ought to take a special pride in lavishing their greatest typographical care on the largest editions of the classical authors.

Possessing the great works of literature in handy pocket size is one of the pleasures of life; and for many centuries the classics have been so produced. In the Middle Ages industrious monks copied out the Bible in tiny script on the thinnest parchment, of pocket size, to make as small a single volume as possible. As soon as printers learned how to cut small types, the first printed pocket editions appeared. But the editions which Aldus Manutius printed of his pocket volumes were not much greater than those of his normal books. Probably the first really large editions of pocket volumes were the famous Elzevirs, which as texts are as useful today as they ever were, besides being typographic master-pieces. It is not yet proved that we can today print such small formats with perfect legibility; modern publishers and readers seem surprisingly prejudiced against these small sizes.

The Didot pocket volumes must have been produced in very large editions, for they were printed from stereotyped plates. Their format, although very attractive, was rather larger than that of the Elzevirs; their typesetting was meticulous, of a standard of excellence since lost not only in France; their textual authority was a by-word. But from the mid-nineteenth century the quality of typesetting fell lower and lower. Spacing between words was increased excessively, and the arrangement of title-pages and headings was more and more neglected.

Sixty years ago in Germany, editions of the classics were unpleasing in appearance, and seemed designed rather to put readers off than to attract them. They were printed on ugly, shiny, ill-tinted yellow-grey or grey-white paper, in the thin, anaemic types of the late nineteenth century. The setting was careless, the type usually too small and not easily legible, the leading insufficient, and the pages overcrowded. Headings were set in particularly ugly types; title-pages lacked any typographical feeling. These feeble specimens of nineteenth-century typography were also of unhandy format, and bound in a way that today makes us shudder.

The Everyman Library and the World's Classics were among the earliest modern attempts to produce the classics in a more worthy form, turning to practical use the movement started by William Morris and his followers to reform book typography. To make them pocket editions, a new thin Bible paper was used, enabling a volume to run to six or seven hundred pages without becoming unwieldy. The Insel thin-paper editions, and the French 'Editions de la Pléiade' are faithful copies of English models.

These new series appealed immediately to the educated public, who were tired of the pretentious decoration and unnecessary size of the editions of classics then current, and found that these new and handsome-looking volumes were about half the size and weight of their predecessors. They have hardly been bettered since in their kind. In fact, little room has been left for improvement, except perhaps in the typography and the decoration of the binding.

The type used, Old Style, is now old-fashioned; and lettering on title-pages, even if by Eric Gill, does not harmonize so well with the rest of a printed book (just because the lettering is so perfect) as would a title-page carefully set in the same type used for the body of the book. The covers of these books are not entirely pleasing today, because they reveal too clearly the signs of the period of their origin.

The format (17·3 by 10·4 cm, 6$\frac{13}{16}$ by 4$\frac{1}{8}$ in.) corresponds exactly to the Golden Mean, and is undoubtedly the best format for pocket editions. It has been adopted with slight alterations for many similar series. All variations consisting of making the pages broader or narrower seem to me ugly and pointless. Format and type area cannot be protected by copyright, and no publisher need fear a lawsuit if he copies exactly the dimensions of a good page from another publisher. Perhaps in no other craft does it so often pay to follow tradition.

The aim of pocket editions is to get as much as possible into as small a space as possible, and narrow margins and cramped type areas can be forgiven, so long as the type used it not too small nor too widely spaced.

When these early thin-paper editions first appeared, Old Style was the best type-face available. But to use it nowadays as a standard face for a pocket edition would be wrong. Thanks largely to the efforts of Mr Stanley Morison, we now have such a large range of fine types to choose from, that it is possible to find exactly the right face for nearly every kind of book.

The typographer who now has all these types to choose from must understand and appreciate the unique character of each. And as the complexity of book-production and the number of specialized processes increase, so does the need, when a book is to be perfectly produced, for a typographer who can design every detail of size, setting, paper and binding; who can be, in fact, a true architect of the book. He must know every subtle effect and modulation to be gained by every possible variation in layout, in style of type, and in spacing. He must have a profound understanding of the nature of the type he is using, and he must be capable, not only of general direction, but of controlling every detail of the physical construction of a book. Only then will beautiful books be produced.

It is the close setting with the lines leaded that distinguishes a good modern edition from an old one. Close setting binds the words together in lines and greatly increases the legibility and beauty of a page. The typographer must use the accumulated experience of typographic history when giving instructions about chapter-openings, or paragraphing, or the layout of plays or poetry. Only the most careful and critical study of the best typography of the past will enable him to notice the details that make such a difference to the whole. The form of the running title, the folio numbering, and, not least, the proportions of the margins, are all questions of great importance.

The further specialization is carried, and the less the compositor's brain is given to do, the more essential does it become for the typographer to go over every page, almost line for line, before he passes it.

The choice of paper also demands the greatest care. White paper should be used when the type is heavily leaded and the type-face belongs to the vertical-stress family,[1] for instance Bodoni, Walbaum or Didot. In all other circumstances, a slightly off-white is better. White paper is tiring to the eyes. Unfortunately, it seems that not a few printers and publishers think that the whiter a paper is, the better it is. This is an error, though not a new one. It seems to have originated with the contemporaries of the Didots and Bodoni, at a period when many papers used for cheap book-production really were too dark. The eye definitely finds it easier to read on slightly toned paper.

It is often necessary to produce a book in sheets of thirty-two pages, and this large number of pages can result in serious errors in folding which can be minimized only by using papers that are not too bulky. If the type-face to be used is one of the Venetian or Aldine group,[2] then the paper surface must definitely be machine finished.

Since the paper for large editions is always specially made, the experienced book-designer's stipulations about colour, surface and weight can easily be met. At a later stage, care must be taken to insist on the book being printed with the paper

[1] Using the term proposed by Mrs B. Warde in *The Library*, September, 1935.
[2] Using the term proposed by Mrs B. Warde, *ibid.*

running the right way, i.e. with the laid lines parallel to the spine, and in the case of wove paper, the grain should likewise run parallel to the spine.

Even quite cheap paper can be distinctly improved by judicious tinting. The weight can also be adjusted, so that volumes of varying length can be produced in approximately uniform thickness.

The best binding for modern series of classics is whole cloth. The Birkhäuser (Basle) series, for the design of which I am responsible, was originally launched in half-cloth, but the public did not find this form of binding wholly satisfactory; in consequence they now appear in whole cloth. The cloth should be neither too coarse nor too light, and should be proof against dust and fingermarks.

Whether gold is really best for printing the title on the spine and the front cover is difficult to decide. Possibly in ten years or so we will find to our shame that even our best gold leaf has oxidized. My own opinion is that either real gold should be used (for expensive editions) or that the cases should be made of smooth, not too dark, cloth, which can be printed on in colours by letterpress or offset, like the binding of Mr Oliver Simon's *Introduction to Typography*. Coloured foil inks are transitory and often ugly, and should never be used in good quality productions. They are unsuitable for use on book materials, and wear off.

Whether books should be flexible or not depends entirely on their format. Only pocket editions should be flexible. It is flexibility which turns a pocket format into a genuine pocket edition. Books larger than Everyman or Penguin size should have stiff bindings, for in them flexibility is neither useful nor desirable. It goes without saying that all books, especially flexible books, should have slightly rounded spines, which prevent the middle pages losing shape after reading. Books with flat spines are an ugly and uncraftsmanlike invention, which no sound book designer would countenance; and they damage the pocket.

The pocket edition is symptomatic of the overcrowding and eternal house-changing of our time, not least when it contains some text of lasting value. But it does not follow that all editions of the classics should be pocket size: one exception is the great critical editions. And, because a book is larger than pocket size, it need not be unwieldy: it can, and should, be correctly proportioned. neither too thick nor too heavy. All our books tend to be too heavy. One has to handle a Chinese book to discover how light paper may be.

Good proportions for trimmed page sizes are 3:5 and 5:8. The Birkhäuser Classics are proportioned 5:8 (19·2 by 12 cm, $7\frac{9}{16}$ by $4\frac{3}{4}$ in.). A very beautiful edition of the works of Prosper Mérimée, printed by Jakob Hegner, has the 3:5

proportion (18·8 by 12·2 cm, 6$\frac{13}{32}$ by 4$\frac{7}{16}$ in.). When a book becomes too wide in proportion to its length, it will not lie easily in the hand: the law of leverage makes it more difficult to hold than a narrower book of the same weight. People read the classics in their leisure time, so that editions of the classics must be suitable for holding in the unsupported hand. Larger books, of what may be called 'table size', do not come within the scope of the present discussion. The typography of non-pocket editions is not subject to the laws of economy which apply to the pocket edition.

I find it consoling, in these days when civilization appears to be tottering, to think that the great tradition of European book-printing has been revived by a few faithful men and is now in our hands, to carry on and, even in the changed conditions of modern mass-production, to improve, if we go to our task with enough seriousness and sense of responsibility. Where could such qualities be more desirable than in the work of passing on the wisdom of the great poets and thinkers by means of books available to Everyman?

Appendix 5 : My reform of Penguin Books

Mein Reform der Penguin Books
Schweizer Graphische Mitteilungen, No.6, 1950

[A few excisions have been made of matter either duplicated elsewhere or now irrelevant.]

Penguin Books are probably, after Hutchinson, the biggest English publisher: they produce about 15 million books a year (at the lowest possible prices); there are about sixteen titles every month, in editions of from 50,000 to 100,000. They do not own either a printing works or a bindery. Furthermore, present circumstances compel them to hold their complete stock in their own warehouse, an average of 8 to 10 million books at any one time.

The man who controls typographical design in an English publishing house is called the typographer. The typographer's communication with printers and binders is by letter. Penguin Books use a large number of printing and binding firms all over the British Isles. Distances are so great that visits even to a firm in London are only occasionally possible: any visit takes nearly a whole day, most of which is spent in travelling. Corrections can hardly ever be made quickly. In exceptional circumstances, they may be made within a week, but more often it takes weeks or even months before one can see a revise. These delays do not make a typographer's life any easier. But now, along came a man who not only wanted nearly everything changed, but also, in this most conservative of countries, produced an entirely new set of typographical rules!

After only a few days in my new job, I saw how urgent it was to establish strict rules for composition. The printers who set the type either had no composition rules at all, or worked to nineteenth-century conventions, or followed one set or another of house rules. Luckily, even in England, the machine compositors can be directed and are ready to follow good composition rules: I had hardly any problems with them, and after about a year (the production of a single book often takes as long, or longer) I could see the improvement in straightforward composition as a result of my *Penguin Composition Rules*, which ran to four printed pages. Although the general practice in both England and Scotland, was, as it had been in the nineteenth century, wide spacing between words and preferably no leading at all between the lines, I insisted on close spacing and leading. I also insisted on the use of the en-dash, with the word space of the line on each side, instead of the em-dash set solid, which greatly improved the appearance of the page. Finally, the practice of putting extra space after full points had to be abolished. These were only the most obvious rules: my list of rules covered a mass of other details.

If it was comparatively easy to persuade the machine compositors to accept these (for Britain) apparently revolutionary rules, with the hand compositors I came up against a stone wall. They simply could not understand what I meant by 'capitals must be letter-spaced'. Because every day I had to wade through miles of corrections (often ten books daily) I had a rubber stamp made: 'Equalize letter-spaces according to their visual value'. It was totally ignored; the hand compositors continued to space out the capitals on title-pages (where optical spacing is essential) with spaces of equal thickness. Because in England there is no commonly accepted correction mark for 'space in' or 'space out', I was forced literally thousands of times to mark between every individual capital, for example, '$\frac{1}{2}$ pt in' or '2 pts out'. That a good hand compositor should always look carefully at capitals and space them by eye is in Britain (as opposed to the USA) entirely unheard of or at least never done. Compositors do not seem to be interested in their work. Printers have told me that compositors who try to produce better results get into severe trouble with their colleagues. So, with everything set by hand – titles, decorations, capital letters and advertisements – I had terrible difficulties, that would never have occurred in Switzerland.

Things began to improve towards the end of my time there, in the summer of 1949. Probably my layouts were generally given to the same compositors, and they eventually began to understand what I wanted. For this reason my layouts had to be far more exact than would be necessary in Switzerland. I had to specify not only the amount of letter-spacing but also the word spacing; if I did not do this, I infallibly got monstrously wide word spacing, which is for me the clearest proof of incompetence in the composing room. The shortcomings of English compositors – whose apprenticeship lasts a full seven years – are in sharp contrast with the opportunities offered by the splendid range of type-faces which have been available on English composing machines for more than twenty years. Fine type-faces, bad composition and appalling hand composition, are the characteristics of the average English printing house of today. The difference between the best English printing (e.g. Oliver Simon at the Curwen Press) and the average is very great – far greater than in Switzerland or the USA. It would be wrong to draw any inference from the one to the other, but unfortunately this fallacy is often committed when one thinks of English typography. While I was in England, I learned to appreciate the value of our own Further Education Courses and Trade Training Schemes in Switzerland.

As the designer responsible for the appearance of all Penguin books, I had to design specimen pages both for the reprints of books already published, and for new titles, as well as chapter openings and advertisement pages at the backs of books; covers had to be either specified typographically or designed entirely *de novo,* corrections for every book had to be examined typographically page by page, and many other tasks that were part of my job had to be attended to. This was such a gigantic task that I soon needed a full-time assistant. Only someone who has been concerned with all the minutiae and time-consuming attention to detail required of a publisher's typographer can begin to appreciate what was involved.

After my Composition Rules had been laid down and circulated, I moved on to the general appearance of Penguin books. They were then nearly all set in Times New Roman, a type outstandingly suitable for newspapers but much less so for books. Of the books I personally supervised, only about twenty per cent are still set in Times New Roman; the rest are now set in Baskerville, Bembo, Garamond and Caslon. In some of the King Penguin series, which resemble the illustrated Inselbücherei, I used more unusual type-faces, for example Pastonchi, Scotch Roman, Lutetia and Walbaum. These type-faces, mostly of classical origin, combined with the new composition rules, and a carefully considered overall re-styling, completely altered the appearance of Penguins.

Title-pages suffered from the heaviness of the Penguin symbol. This had gradually become more and more corrupted, and I had to find a new solution which would match up to the original design, which was good.

I redrew the Penguin in about eight different variations. For title-pages I designed some decorated swelled rules. The versos of title-pages, so often neglected by typographers, were a special concern of mine. That a solution can be found for even such a difficult problem as this, is shown by the illustration.

Finally, I had to work on designs for the covers of various series. I produced a successful new design for the covers of Pelican Books, the scientific and educational series, and a new design of mine for the main Penguin series, with a few alterations, is at the moment under discussion.

Up till now it has not been possible to alter the old flag-like division of Penguin covers: all I could do was to improve the proportions and replace the deformed symbol. Because the present standard Penguin cover is not entirely my own work, I do not reproduce it here. I do however show cover designs, which are entirely my own work, for *The Centuries' Poetry*, *A Dictionary of Geography*, *The Penguin Shakespeare* and *Penguin Music Scores*.

In addition, I had to oversee countless children's books, and besides their text pages to keep an eye on the typography of their covers, often an exhausting and sometimes a thankless task. From the middle of 1948 I had a young Dane, Erik Frederiksen, as my very congenial and hard-working assistant.

After a long struggle I finally won my battle for the correct direction of the paper, previously neglected, and for a slightly cream colour instead of the previous dirty grey.

Gradually the results of my work began to be noticeable.

In 29 months, I designed or prepared for press more than 500 books, mostly page by page, which must be nearly a world record. Eventually the work began to get easier, as the origination had been mostly done, and many things became a matter of routine.

Then, in September 1949, the English pound was heavily devalued, and I was compelled to return to Switzerland, a little earlier than I had expected. But I am glad to be able to say that my task at Penguins was already completed. I am also glad that my work is being well taken care of by H. P. Schmoller, a first-class book designer, and its fundamental lines can now hardly be altered. The firm of Penguins is assured that its books, produced as cheaply as possible in millions for the millions, are every bit as well set and designed as the most expensive in the country – indeed, better than most!

Appendix 6 : Letters written by Jan Tschichold to Alfred Fairbank

8 April 1949

Dear Fairbank,

Thank you for your interesting letter of 5 April and its many questions. I will do my best to give you satisfactory answers to all these.

When I said that good typography was a science rather than an art I meant that it depended on knowledge, a knowledge growing out of experience. On the other hand art, in my article, is conceived more as something growing from the unconscious. I am convinced that no one is a born calligrapher or typographer: both need very great experience before they become real masters.

I was taught by my father, who is a sign writer, in painting letters, but when I made at 17, my first design for typography, a letter paper for my father's business, I felt quite disappointed with the result, not because it was not what I wanted but because it was not good: in other words I could not do it. Afterwards I tried to find laws – and now at 47 I am still searching for genuine and readily understood rules, for the arrangement of letters. Maybe there are such rules but they are elusive, as they are, as a rule, derived from result and not from an idea.

One reason for this incapability of doing my father's letter paper was the surroundings of my youth. At that time Germany suffered (unconsciously) from that style which is called in England 'Victorian'. General lettering, and also book typography, was in a deplorable state, and I still remember how I substituted the title-page of a cheap edition of a favourite author of my youth, the German poet Clemens Brentano, by another which I designed very carefully by using careful replicas of the standard types which had stood the test of time. But, like every beginner, I had no real understanding for the arrangement of letters, as little, in fact, as any ordinary compositor.

Afterwards I taught myself calligraphy, by following Johnston and Larisch and was also taught, to a certain degree, by Professor H. Delitsch. I executed several MSS and taught at 18, calligraphy in the evening classes of the Leipzig Academy. For a calligrapher, as a rule, the problems of letter arrangement are not so complicated as they are for a typographer. The number of problems in a hand-written book is smaller than in a modern printed one, but I feel there is no better training for a typographer than practical calligraphy.

All my knowledge of letter-spacing, word-spacing and leading is due to my calligraphy, and for this reason I regret very much that calligraphy is so little studied in our time among so-called book artists. For instance, no calligrapher can ever approve letter-spaced lower cases and the original feeling of a calligrapher about letter-spacing is certainly a good guide for letter-spacing in every kind of typography. Anyone who has ever done lettering by hand knows much more about the qualities of right spacing than a mere compositor who only hears certain rules without understanding them. I admire the English sign writers' works, but generally speaking I despise the English hand compositors' work.

The sentence: 'The rules for correct letterspacing are usually well taught, but all too frequently they are not followed', is actually a suggestion of Mr Fishenden in place of a much stronger formulation that I had before. The original version was something like this: 'The right rules for correct letterspacing can be found rather easily as they are put down in several text books, but unfortunately they are not followed.'

Calligraphy is taught, but typography is not; this is true if we mean the art of typography. In the whole world all real typographers are self-taught people, though maybe in the next generation there will be a few disciples of the living typographers. Typography is taught only technically, at least in England and in several other countries, and this is the reason why the average typography as in newspapers, catalogues, leaflets and the great majority of books, is so lamentable. Too little attention is given to the right letter and word-spacing and to the arrangement of the lines within their area. It is not because people are unable to do this in a better way; they are not taught, and therefore not really interested in such things. As soon as individual compositors are taught about the possible qualities of their work many of them will be keen to apply the rules.

The relation between sign writers and compositors in Switzerland is just the opposite to what it is here. Compositors are good: sign writers are bad. However, after having published my little work *Gute Schriftformen*, which was mainly intended as a guide for sign writers, there was an increasing improvement of all public signs in Basle, and also in other Swiss towns, applying the letter forms I gave in this book. This seems to me a testimonial for the possibility of improvement either of sign writing or of typography. It is always the actual performance which convinces, and it is also the actual performance of the books I produced in Switzerland which had that widespread influence on Swiss typography.

But now I should come back to some of your other questions. The importance of the fact that the tops of letters are more important than the bottoms has no significance where letter-spacing is concerned. In comparing letter-spaces we see the whole shape of the letters, and not only the upper part of them. I cannot establish any permanent rule for the amount of space between caps in comparison with their depth. This is a matter of the artistic conception of the whole page. I can only make the general assertion that the more space there is around the line the bigger the letter-spaces may be. If there is no space then letter-spaces should be proportionately small.

So much for letter-spacing in general. But letter-spacing has still another meaning, and this is equalizing the letter-spaces in lines of caps. Here many sins are committed every day by every compositor, and I think this aspect of it has been neglected by compositors. As I have written above sign writers do marvellous work here.

You certainly know the doctrine of R. v. Larisch, or do you? This doctrine had a big influence on the development of the lettering and calligraphy in Germany, I dare say the same as Johnston's stimulations. Therefore it is hard to find serious mistakes now in letter-spacing either in Germany, in Switzerland or in Hungary. One of the cover pages of my book mentioned above contains rules for letter-spacing particularly derived from Larisch, but also containing some extensions of those rules, so I may refer to that page. Larisch overlooked the difficulty of balancing an 'o' in a line while I established a rule to have a space round an 'o' balancing the interior part of the letter with its surroundings, otherwise an 'o' looks like a hole.

In ending this letter I see that perhaps not everything I have said is a real answer to your questions, but maybe this gives you, if not an answer, stimulation for further discussion.
Yours,

(signed) Jan Tschichold
I am sorry I have not answered several of your questions – may I postpone this until a later letter?

20 April 1949

Dear Fairbank,

Thank you for your letter of the 10th. Firstly I have much pleasure in sending you the unfinished design for the cover of your book. As I was not satisfied with the reproduction of Perpetua caps I have designed special letters for the lettering of which I enclose an enlarged photograph. The actual size will be the same as in the unfinished drawing. I personally think the design will be successful, and I hope you will like it.

It is really not easy to establish exact rules about spacing of caps. The only general rule which should be observed whenever possible is to produce a rhythmical sequence. The width of the optical letter-spacing is a matter of taste and, I dare say, of an attitude to life. The Renaissance, for instance, had a preference for rather wide letter-spaces not only in the small sizes, but also in the larger ones, and to balance this they also used considerably wider distances between the lines (called by the printer 'lead').

This was observed until the end of the eighteenth century. In the nineteenth century the original feeling for lettering was gradually lost. This, I believe, was the natural outcome of the later eighteenth-century approach to geometrically designed letters, and a merely rationalistic attitude both to our letter design and word-spacing. Word-spacing was considerably widened, while the rhythmical balance of the letter-spaces became more and more neglected.

It was not until Morris and Johnston that a few people began at last to revive the feeling for the need of well balanced letter-spacing but, unfortunately, not so much among the printers but among letterers and sign-writers. Printers in general still have to learn a lot in this respect. The majority of them obviously have to learn to acquire the knowledge of well balanced letter-spacing quite apart from the right use of individual manners of letter-spacing in a given book.

As the proportional amount of letter-spacing depends upon the style of type and the stylistic attitude of the book, it is practically impossible to establish rules. If they did exist they would be so complicated that no normal compositor could follow them. The result of such an investigation, therefore, is that correct letter-spacing is the most personal skill of the letterer, compositor or sign-writer, and their work is evidence of their acquaintance with these confusing rules.

The same does not apply to word-spacing, however. I believe that close word-spacing, which is favoured by nearly all letterers and the best typographers, is – perhaps strangely – the expression of a more or less religious attitude to life. I base my opinion on the extremely close word-spacing in the fifteenth and sixteenth century, and on the comparatively wide word-spacing in the 'materialistic' nineteenth century. It is doubtful whether our age is more religious than the nineteenth century, but certainly a few people – and I feel the letterers might be among them – observe a religion. Some of them may, perhaps, protest against this statement, but they will certainly agree that, as true artists, they see life as a whole, and conceive their work either consciously or unconsciously as a symbol of the right attitude to life or of the idea of human behaviour and view. It is true that a number of readers of books will not agree to close composition. This would prove that they still have the nineteenth-century attitude. Here the typographer or letterer can, perhaps, prepare this part of the public for a life surrounded by genuine and noble creations of Man.

Yours sincerely,

(signed) Jan Tschichold

22 August 1949

My dear Fairbank,

Thank you for your letter of the 19th August. You seem to be uncertain whether I had really corrected p.39 in accordance with your wishes. I have now checked this again and can assure you that your addition to the third paragraph was included.

As you had no advice about the size of your plates you could not know that there are limitations. Very soon after my coming to England I had to design a maximum area for the King Penguins, a specimen of which I enclose. Such a maximum area is important for the look of the plates as much as it is a guarantee for the harmony of ordinary text pages. Your measures very often exceeded these possibilities, and so I had either to trim or to reduce them. In a book of such a small size as the King Penguins, certain compromises are unfortunately unavoidable.

I quite agree that the comparison between plate 8 and plate 56 is under the present circumstances not too easy but there is no help I am afraid now. Very sorry.

Very often I have wanted to tell you how much I am always pleased to get a letter from you sealed with another of your beautiful seals. I guess you have a rather large collection of such Georgian seals. I appreciate this very much and I have collected them with care.

All good wishes,

Yours,

(signed) Jan Tschichold

P.S. Thank you for returning the cover. Fortunately I got in the meantime another pull so you can have it now.

21 November 1949

My dear Fairbank,

Thank you for your letters of the 1st and 6th November. I am glad you enjoyed the typography of your book which has already had, I understand, a very great success in London.

I enjoyed the execution of your book very much and this the more as the book as a whole became a sort of little monument of our mutual friendship.

Ever yours,

(signed) Jan Tschichold

Appendix 7: Letter written by Jan Tschichold to Rudolf Hostettler, St Gallen

31 January 1946

Dear Herr Hostettler,

I have been overburdened and so unable to answer your kind letter of the 3 January until now. And I can only answer your letter briefly because it is concerned with complicated matters that will be best dealt with by word of mouth when a suitable occasion arises. I will now try to answer your questions in an abbreviated way.

Only for a second does my comparison of the New Typography with National Socialism appear paradoxical. Very many people were driven out of Germany who were indeed enemies of National Socialism but were still exponents of a German style. In the last resort, however, all extreme Germanism ends up as National Socialism. That I myself was hushed up by the German writers in my subject during the Nazi era does not constitute evidence to the contrary.

Absence of compromise is only one side of a revolution; the question always is, what principles underlie it. If one comes to recognize that the principles are extreme, absence of compromise is no longer of value.

It is true that the New Typography has gone on developing and has shed the inflexible dogmas of the early days. Asymmetrical typography is by no means obsolete and in the field of advertising is a great step forward. It is by no means a thing of the past. Many elements of the New Typography have been taken over into the modern centred setting as you too practise it.

Obviously one can point to visible traces of the New Typography in the work of the graphic artists whom you mention. As in general the artists of a period influence one another consciously or unconsciously. Thus in my opinion even E. R. Weiss is influenced by the New Typography. All the same, it will not do to classify the New Typography as Bauhaus Typography. For Bauhaus Typography has not developed beyond its beginnings. If Zerbe teaches wholly in the spirit of my manuals or has taken crucial ideas from me, the fact that he does not mention my name simply means that he wishes to deny his dependence upon me. The New Typography made itself felt in America earlier than it did in England. I did not begin to be known in England until about 1936; I designed a volume of the *Penrose Annual* at that time. The commercial art of the eighteenth century has not gone on evolving quite as calmly in England as we are inclined to think from here. The average quality of advertising typography is much poorer there than it is here, or than it was in Germany earlier on. (In Germany since 1933 typography and the so-called applied graphic arts have gone further and further downhill because creative talents were suppressed or went abroad. An interesting proof of this is the last special number of the *Leipziger Illustrierte* (Christmas 1944, I think), the advertisement section of which looks as though it has been printed in the year 1923, although pretty well only four-colour blocks were used for it.)

It has yet to be proved whether an understanding of the New Typography can be realized painlessly in England without the wrong turnings that we took. At all events, the English are at present extremely interested in the New Typography and want to publish no fewer than three books of mine that deal with the subject. So they obviously stand where I stood in 1932.

In my lecture I was, I admit, thinking primarily of book typography; nevertheless, my representations may be understood to show that even typography designed for books is valid for jobbing printing and should be cultivated more widely. The position today is that neither symmetrical nor asymmetrical setting can be regarded as the 'ideal'; the typographer will move in one direction or the other according to his assignment.

The Monotype re-cuttings are on the whole extraordinarily careful and only in very minor details have they been modified to the requirements of machine technique.

A book on the history of the Bauhaus and kindred trends has appeared at the Museum of Modern Art in New York, but I do not recall its title. However, it does not deal so much with the private lot of the earlier teachers.

A lecture by Bertram Evans on the New Typography is cited in the bibliography of Tarr's book. I have not yet had a sight of the volume, but I will have it sent.

Many thanks for sending the numbers of the *Schweizerische Graphische Mitteilungen*. Unfortunately I have not finished going through my earlier writings, though I shall do so in the course of the coming week. In the meantime I am sending you, together with a few numbers of the *SGM* which I already possess and had mentioned to you in error, an incomplete run of the Munich school Newsletters, which may be of interest to you.

Please do not look for any further numbers, I assure you that I am satisfied. For myself the most interesting thing was your valuable article on type specimens in March 1944, on the fourth page of which I am glad to see that you quoted my views from the August 1938 number.

With kind regards,

Jan Tschichold

Appendix 8: Quousque Tandem ...

Talk given by Jan Tschichold to the Type Directors Club, New York on 18 April 1959 Subsequently printed in *Print*, XVIII, No.1, New York, 1964

Although you will consider what is to follow as Chinese thinking, I can assure you I am no Chinese. Nor am I a white elephant, in spite of the very few hairs on my head. I am alive and active, although many of my friends would be doubtful about this since I am, alas, probably the laziest correspondent in the world. After having been asked so often for a contribution to the activities of the Type Directors Club of New York, and in order not to be erroneously considered a solitary, may I offer you, in all modesty, a few of my opinions about Typography.

In Switzerland a few years ago, there was a rumour too about the possibilities of a 'Swiss' typography. I do not believe in the value of any 'national' typography. The attempt to create a 'national' typography certainly is, to my mind, a fallacy. Still, even when such an approach is expressly avoided, it is in practice often the casual result of work. In general, we should consider the typography of the Western world as one and the same thing. True, we can no more overlook the English approach than the American one, and probably nobody will be doubtful that there is a certain Swiss approach of today. The latter, for which I do not feel responsible, is the exemplar of a most inflexible typography which makes no distinction between the advertising of an artistic performance or of a screw catalogue. Nor does this typography allow for the human desire for variety. It has an entirely militaristic attitude.

What I do today is not in the line of my often mentioned book *Die neue Typographie*, since I am the most severe critic of the young Tschichold of 1925–8. A Chinese proverb says 'In haste there is error'. So many things in that primer are erroneous, because my experience was too small.

In Germany in 1925 (and the present situation there is not too different from that period), far too many type-faces were used and, with a few exceptions, only bad ones. (I still remember the deep satisfaction of the moment when I saw, by chance, at the tender age of seventeen, English magazine pages set up in Caslon.)

Those German type-faces appeared in undisciplined arrangements, not at all 'traditional' in the present-day meaning of this word. Those unacquainted with it can hardly imagine the mediocrity of German typography of that period. As a letterer, I felt insulted day after day by the ugly appearance of the newspapers, magazines and the many sorts of advertisements. To cure these weaknesses I suggested two remedies, one for the type and one for the arrangement.

In order to reduce the number of type-faces, German as I was then, I thought the solution to be in a single type-face only, for all purposes, namely that which is called in German *Grotesk*, in English *Sanserif*, and in the States *Gothic*. For the arrangement I suggested total asymmetry instead of centring the lines.

Now I have to reveal what I think is wrong with these juvenile ideas and with the situation of 1924. It was not the great number of type-faces in fashion then, but the poor quality of practically all these type-faces; and it was not the general unsuitability of a centred order but the lack of the compositor's skill in such arrangements. Had I been more experienced then than could be expected at the age of 23, and had I been instructed in arranging type (of which I never heard lectures in my youth nor later because there weren't any available), then perhaps I should have thought over my immature ideas more carefully.

So far, in this haste, there was error. Yet, very often, error is creative. My errors were more fertile than I ever imagined. Certainly the typography of the time shortly before 1925 was, in general, ailing, and in urgent need of a doctor. The treatment was heroic but healthy. Yet one cannot live by abstinence and pharmaceutics. The weakness of the period before 1925 was the lack of at least one good type. It would have been better to look out for a good type, or better, for a greater number of useful type-faces than to reduce their number to a single type-face of doubtful utility. In the light of my present knowledge, it was a juvenile opinion to consider the sanserif as the most suitable or even the most contemporary type-face. A type-face has first to be legible, nay, readable, and a sanserif is not the most legible type-face when set in quantity, let alone readable. Nor does a centred arrangement of too many different and even ugly letters prove the inappropriateness of line centring in general, but lack of skill and artistic intelligence.

A few years after *Die neue Typographie* Hitler came. I was accused of creating 'un-German' typography and art, and so I preferred to leave Germany. Since 1933 I have lived in Basle, Switzerland. In the very first years I tried to develop what I had called *Die neue Typographie* and wrote another text-book, *Typographische Gestaltung* in 1935 which is much more prudent than *Die neue Typographie* and still a useful book! In time, typographical things, in my eyes, took on a very different aspect, and to my astonishment I detected most shocking parallels between the teachings of *Die neue Typographie* and National Socialism and Fascism. Obvious similarities consist in the ruthless restriction of type-faces, a parallel to Goebbels' infamous *gleichschaltung*, and the more or less militaristic arrangement of lines. Because I did not want to be guilty of spreading the very ideas which had compelled me to leave Germany I thought over again what a typographer should do. Which type-faces are good and what arrangement is the most practicable? By guiding the compositors of a large Basle printing office I learnt a lot about practicability. Good typography has to be perfectly legible and is, as such, the result of intelligent planning. The classical type-faces such as Garamond, Janson, Baskerville and Bell are undoubtedly the most legible. Sanserif is good for certain cases of emphasis, but is used to the point of abuse today. The occasions for using sanserif are as rare as those for wearing obtrusive decorations.

Every asymmetrical arrangement needs its own individual design. Asymmetry is a secret known to a group of initiates and not easy for the average compositor to acquire. He learns to push a line to the left or to the right: never centre it! True, a perfectly symmetrical arrangement is not easy. This in no way invalidates the principle, however, and no assymmetrist is entitled to blame it for this difficulty since his own arrangements lack even common sense; and the most slavish compositor will in time lose all pleasure in such work. A centred typography, while certainly not suitable for all purposes, is comparatively simple, and even the inexperienced compositor without intelligent guidance, cannot commit grave faults there.

Unfortunately this bad, austere, rigid typography still persists, especially in the town where I live. Is the typographer a prophet or a propagator of a new faith?

Typography should be allowed individuality; this is to appear as different as the people around us, just as there are girls and men, fat and thin, wise and stupid, serious and gay, easily pleased and fussy.

The aim of typography must not be expression, least of all self-expression, but perfect communication achieved by skill. Taking over working principles from previous times or other typographers is not wrong but sensible. Typography is a servant and nothing more. The servant Typography ought to be the most perfect servant.

Our needs change and for this reason alone the attitude of typography may also change slightly. Our eyes, however, do not change. They are still the same organ as Garamond had. As printed matter sometimes (we hope, in the most deserving cases) survives its originators and what we plan today may be read 200 years hence, just as we can read books printed 300 years ago, typography must not change very much. Essentially dependent on the shape of letters, it is an example of genuine tradition. Probably nowhere else is so little change noticeable and necessary as in typography.

The term used to characterize such activities as my own of today, traditionalism, deserves a short consideration. It is definitely not a natural continuation of the typography before 1925, and has, in fact, practically nothing to do with it. That tradition, if it was one, was dead. The few who work today in the same way as I do, had to regain by hard labour another healthy tradition which is neither the useless repetition nor imitation of the sixteenth or eighteenth century manner nor a blind revival of obsolete rules. It uses all the contemporary possibilities and responds to all needs. A draughtsman or a compositor of the nineteenth century could hardly comply with modern tastes.

After having spoken most critically about my own early work and after having bored you with so many personal remarks, I want to use this opportunity to pay tribute to the outstandingly high quality of typography in the United States. Even if you yourselves deny it, I as a historian must assert that it has a history as long and glorious as that of the States. The happy unity of language of almost a whole continent allowing for huge printings, in combination with your unlimited technical possibilities and last, and by no means least, the presence of so many highly-gifted individual typographers, often produces printed matter of paramount quality which I admire.

INDEX